LONDON
STREET NAMES

Edited by
Michael Baker with Hilary Bates Neary

Hellmuth Avenue showing Church of St. John the Evangelist,
London, Ont. Canada.

St. James Street.

James Lorimer & Company Ltd., Publishers
Toronto

James Lorimer & Company Ltd. acknowledges the support of the Ontario Arts Council. We acknowledge the support of the Government of Canada, through the Book Publishing Industry Development Programs (BPIDP), for our publishing activities. We acknowledge the support of the Canada Council for the Arts for our publishing program. We acknowledge the support of the Government of Ontario through the Ontario Media Development Corporation's Ontario Book Initiative.

National Library of Canada Cataloguing in Publication

Baker, Michael, 1959 Oct. 5-
    London street names : an illustrated guide / Michael Baker with Hilary Bates Neary.

Includes index.
ISBN 1-55028-802-4

    1. Street names—Ontario—London—Pictorial works. 2. London (Ont.)—History—Pictorial works. I. Neary, Hilary Bates, 1946- II. Title.

FC3099.L65Z56 2003   971.3'26   C2003-903620-0

Photo Credits:
Legend: Top — T; Bottom — B; Left — L; Right — R

All visuals provided by Museum London except for those listed below:
Archives of Ontario: 83; Chris Doty: 46; Don Fleckser: 45; Huron University College: 86; Campbell McDonald: 16; National Archives of Canada: 28; The University of Western Ontario Archives, J.J. Talman Regional Collection: 1, 5, 20, 23, 35, 40, 49, 50, 55, 72, 74, 75, 85, 87, 100, 101, 109B, 110; The University of Western Ontario Archives, London Free Press Collection of Photographic Negatives: 7, 38, 65; John Tamblyn Inc.: 10, 11, 21, 25T, 29, 39, 43, 44, 51, 52, 58, 64, 69, 76, 77, 79, 82T, 82B, 84BL, 84B, 88, 89, 91T, 91B, 93, 98, 102, 105, 109T

James Lorimer & Company Ltd., Publishers
35 Britain St.
Toronto, Ontario
M5A 1R7
www.lorimer.ca

Printed and bound in Canada

CONTENTS

Richmond Street looking south toward Dundas Street, circa 1910.

DEDICATION

Dedicated to the developers, their planners and surveyors, and to London's civic officials and their staffs, who have seen fit, on occasion, to use a street to commemorate a person, place or significant event.

Sometimes whimsy or left field give rise to a street name, but more often it comes from the locale and its residents, and after years have passed it is the only reminder of an area, a community, a farm, or a family. Acknowledging that link is a service to the community from which we can know our past.

Tarring cedar blocks on Talbot Street, circa 1890.

INTRODUCTION

London Street Names is a small sample of London's nearly twenty-five hundred streets. Each street was selected for the story behind the individual or location associated with it. Some are but a few years old while others predate the founding of the city. Several have survived from the former municipalities and neighbourhoods that make up present-day London. Many commemorate famous citizens while others perpetuate the names of owners who registered plans of subdivision, or who named a street after an earlier resident. Together they present a series of vignettes from our community's past.

The town plot of London, surveyed in 1826, had a mere fifteen streets. Many of their names were probably selected by Thomas Talbot who controlled the granting of lots in the town, in the surrounding townships, and in counties throughout southwestern Ontario. In his choice of street names Talbot recognized friends, his surveyor, Mahlon Burwell, and several benefactors, Lieutenant-Colonel John Graves Simcoe being one. It is unlikely, however, that the Duke of Clarence or Lord Bathurst knew that streets in a Canadian town bore their names.

The view east along Pipe Line Road (now Springbank Drive) from Reservoir Hill, circa 1900.

Covent Garden Market, looking northeast from Talbot Street, circa 1910.

Another twenty-four streets were added in 1840 when London was incorporated and the boundaries extended from the branches of the Thames to Huron and Adelaide Streets. A tradition of appropriating names from the other London began then and continued throughout the nineteenth century. Oxford, Pall Mall, Piccadilly, and St. James all appeared in 1840. City fathers easily found reasons for using streets to express their loyalty to Great Britain and the Crown. Lorne and Dufferin, for example, were both named for Canadian Governors-General. Battles fought for Crown and empire also inspired street names: Alma and Inkerman survive from the Crimea, Paardeberg from the South African War, and St. Julien from World War I.

From the beginning, London has steadily acquired territory from its two surrounding townships, London and Westminster. As settlement grew, their side roads and concessions acquired both the names of the communities they ran through (or took travellers towards), and those of early settlers who lived on them. Many of these street names have survived subsequent annexations.

Annexation was and is the most frequent cause for changing a street name, because duplicate names (even ones that sounded alike) were always replaced in the annexed areas. Between 1880 and 1898 the outlying suburbs of London East, South, and West were brought into the city. Many names of founding families of these areas disappeared from streets in the process. The loss of these older names may well have been the impetus for Harriett Priddis, around 1905, to begin researching the origin of London's street names. She found sources for about 250 names, representing most of the streets then existing in London.

Her wide knowledge of the community and her acquaintance with many landholding families were beneficial to her detective work. *London Street Names* relies on many clues left in her paper, "The Naming of London Streets" (published in the London and Middlesex Historical Society *Transactions* in 1909), and builds on her work by including many streets named in the twentieth century.

The contributors to *London Street Names* all responded enthusiastically to the request for entries. Some of them have made the study of London's history their life work; others are recognized specialists in their fields; and a few have been in the right place at the right time to witness the creation of new streets. The depth and originality of their contributions and their patience with the process of compiling them into this book are greatly appreciated.

As well, editor and authors alike are grateful for the assistance received from Arthur McClelland and the staff of the London Room,

Looking east from the corner of Richmond and Dundas Streets, September 30, 1950.

London Public Library, and from John Lutman, Theresa Regnier, and Stephen Harding of the J.J. Talman Regional Collection, at The University of Western Ontario. Cheryl Koteles in the City of London Planning Department generously shared her street name files as well as those of her colleague, Denis Hammond, who named a great many streets during his twenty-five years as senior subdivision planner with the city.

I am especially grateful for the painstaking examination of all the submissions by Dan Brock and Glen Curnoe, two of our more prolific contributors. Finally, the success, even the very appearance, of this book was assured when Hilary Bates Neary agreed to assist me with the commissioning and editing of the entries.

Our authors demonstrate a collective interest in the people and places of London streets that will, I trust, make this book a lasting guide to our civic past.

Mike Baker

Dundas Street looking east from Adelaide, circa 1910.

Looking south on Wortley Road from the Post Office on Askin Street, circa 1910.

ASKIN STREET

Old South. Runs east/west between Wortley Road and Wharncliffe Road.

Colonel John Baptiste Askin was born in Detroit in 1788, when it was still under British control. He "took great pride in his descent from the original lords of the forest," being of Native American and Scots-Irish descent. As a young man, he worked in the fur trade for the Hudson's Bay Company.

Askin fought in defence of Canada in the War of 1812. Following the war, he became an assistant commissary officer in the British army. In 1819, he was appointed clerk of the peace for the London District, whose administrative capital was in Vittoria, near Long Point. After the court-house and jail were damaged by fire in November 1825, the district capital was moved to London, and a new court-house built there.

Askin followed, permanently settling in London in 1832.

During the Rebellion of 1837, Askin, a militia colonel, seized the printing press of a radical publication, the St. Thomas *Liberal*. He lived on a 150-acre estate extending from present-day Byron Avenue to Tecumseh Avenue and from Wortley Road to Wharncliffe Road. His house, "Woodview," occupied the northwest corner of Wortley Road and Elmwood Avenue. He died there in 1869. Teresa and Cynthia Streets, which cross Askin, are named after his daughters. Woodview was torn down about 1886.

Glen Curnoe

A T T A W A N D A R O N   R O A D

Northwest. Runs north/south from Aldersbrook Road to the London Museum of Archaeology.

Nestled above the Medway Valley, this area was inhabited as early as the fifteenth century by the Attawandaron people, an Iroquoian-speaking group closely related to the Huron confederacy to the northeast, between Georgian Bay and Lake Simcoe, and the Iroquois confederacy to the east, between present-day Albany and Buffalo, New York. Politically independent of each, the Attawandaron were called the

A reconstructed Attawandaron longhouse.

The village palisade.

Neutrals by the French at the time of European contact in the early seventeenth century. The Huron-Iroquois conflicts of the later 1640s destroyed their society.

At the south end of Attawandaron Road are the remains of a Neutral village which archaeologists began to assess in the late nineteenth century. Ray Lawson, owner of a local printing company, purchased the land in 1920, and allowed archaeologists, including Wilfrid Jury, to explore the area. In 1969, he presented the site to The University of Western Ontario, which relocated its archaeology museum there in 1980. A village longhouse and palisade were recreated and a new London Museum of Archaeology was constructed underground. The Lawson Site remains a working archaeological dig, and an educational resource for students and visitors to London.

Douglas Leighton

BANTING CRESCENT

Northwest. Runs south off Lawson Road.

Banting Crescent's namesake once described London as both "the place of my hours of misery" and "the place where I had the idea that was to change my life, possibly the lives of others." Unable to secure a position at Toronto's Hospital for Sick Children, Dr. Frederick Banting moved to London in July 1920 to establish a private medical practice. Patient numbers did not grow at the pace he expected, and he accepted a position as a demonstrator at the Western University Medical School (as it was then called). After preparing a lecture on diabetes, a subject he admitted knowing little about, Banting retired for the evening. In the early morning of October 31, 1920, he arose from his bed and put to paper a twenty-five word hypothesis, which inspired the research that led to the discovery of insulin the following year. Over the next two years, a team composed of Banting, C.H. Best, J.B. Collip and J.J.R. Macleod produced a form of insulin suitable for human use. It has since saved the lives of millions of people. Banting and Macleod were awarded the 1923 Nobel Prize in Physiology or Medicine and shared their prize money with Best and Collip.

Sir Frederick Banting Secondary School, from which the crescent gets its name, was officially opened in 1969, with the scientist's widow, Lady Henrietta Banting, in attendance. One year later, on the 50th anniversary of the insulin hypothesis, Lady Banting returned to London to unveil a London Public Library Historic Sites plaque at his former home on Adelaide Street, now a National Historic Site.

Grant Maltman

BASE LINE ROAD

South. Runs east/west from Westminster Avenue to Southcrest Drive. In Byron, the road is known as Byron Baseline Road.

Before London was established, London and Westminster Townships were laid out on either side of the Thames River. In 1810, the government authorized Simon Zelotes Watson, a surveyor and settlement agent from Montreal, to survey lots in Westminster and bring in settlers from Lower Canada. Watson ran a single straight line, or "base line," across the township just south of the river from which two

Entrance to the West End of London, *circa 1841, by George R. Dartnell. This view looks north along Western Road near the corner of present-day Platt's Lane.*

ranges, or concessions of lots, were then laid out.

Settlers preferred to build their homes and perform their statutory roadwork on Commissioners Road, which was adjacent to Watson's base line and already open. Thus only two sections of the base line were opened as roads, one in Byron, west of where Commissioners angles northward, and the other in London's Old South neighbourhood, where present-day Base Line Road marks the southern boundary of an 1819 survey of park lots by Mahlon Burwell.

Colonel Thomas Talbot, the area's highly independent government land agent, interfered with Watson's settlement and eventually had it rescinded in 1811. He likely saw Watson as the first of several agents who would compete with him for settlers, whom he needed to open his road system (see **COL. TALBOT ROAD**). Watson, incensed, and likely impoverished by this action, joined the invading Americans the following year who raided the area, burning mills and homesteads.

Dan Brock

BATHURST STREET

Central. Runs east/west from Thames Street to just east of Adelaide Street.

Henry Bathurst, the third Earl Bathurst (1762-1834), was Secretary of State for War and the Colonies from 1812-27, administering the British Empire and directing military policy for about twice as long as anyone else. This he did with a staff of never more than two dozen. His personal authority was thus immense. Although other departments had jurisdiction in the colonies, such as the Treasury, the Ordnance, and the Admiralty, Bathurst was for most colonists synonymous with the British government and is commemorated all over what was then the Empire. A discussion at his office on Downing Street — and even more an invitation to his house at Cirencester — were considered marks of favour by colonists who travelled to Britain. Bathurst decided what resources could be spared for the War of 1812, and his undersecretary, Henry Goulburn, was effectively the chief negotiator of the Treaty of Ghent with the Americans. Bathurst was the final arbiter of colonial quarrels, the granter of lands and other forms of patronage, and the person who appointed governors and many other officials. Among those Bathurst appointed to Canada were Charles Lennox, 4th Duke of Richmond, his brother-in-law (under whom Arthur Wellesley, 1st Duke of Wellington had also served while Richmond was the viceroy of Ireland), and Major-General Sir Peregrine Maitland, one of the heroes of the battle of Waterloo, who married Richmond's daughter, Lady Sarah Lennox, at Wellington's headquarters in 1815. London's street names reflect this familial intimacy.

Neville Thompson

BEAVERBROOK AVENUE

West. Runs north/south between Riverside Drive and Oxford Street West, and east/west between Capulet Lane and Proudfoot Lane.

Max Aitken was born in Maple, northwest of Toronto, on May 25, 1879. When he was 10 months old, his father, a Presbyterian minister, was "called" to St. James Presbyterian Church in Newcastle, New Brunswick. Aitken was full of mischief from the start, and he was on the make. As a young man, he was introduced to R.B. Bennett, lawyer and politician (Prime Minister of Canada from 1930-35), who taught Aitken the value of talent, integrity, and hard work. That didn't always suit Aitken, but he learned the ways of business from Bennett and was always grateful for it. A career in investment banking took him from Halifax to Montreal, then to London, England. In 1910, he was elected to the British House of Commons. By 1916, he was Baron Beaverbrook and sitting in the House of Lords by age 37. He owed his appointment to his Conservative Party connections, which were strengthened through his control of a popular party newspaper, *The Daily Express*. He ran the newspaper by telephone from wherever he happened to be. He insisted on economies, often quixotically, yet was unusually generous to his foreign correspondents. Readability was Aitken's top priority; he was intolerant of dullness in writing or people. He was an excellent expediter, and Churchill made him Minister of Aircraft Production in 1940 at the critical point in the war.

Aitken married Gladys Drury of Halifax in 1904 and led her a fairly rough life. They had three children. She died of a brain tumour in 1927, leaving Max with a guilty conscience. It did not prevent future escapades. He exuded money and power and was attracted to elegant women, and the feeling seems to have been mutual. "That little nut-brown man," as one of his secretaries called him, died in 1964.

P. B. Waite

BECHER STREET

Old South. Runs east/west between the Thames River and Wharncliffe Road.

In the 1850s, Henry Corry Rowley Becher, George Macbeth, George Horn, and Lionel Ridout had a block of land located between the tracks of the Great Western Railway (now the Canadian National Railway) and the Thames River surveyed, and then named the streets after themselves.

Henry Becher was born in London, England, on June 5, 1817. He arrived in London, Upper Canada, in August 1835 with a letter of introduction to Captain John Harris of Eldon House. Following Harris's advice, he articled with the prominent London lawyer John Wilson. He was appointed registrar of the Surrogate Court of Middlesex County in 1839, and called to the bar in 1841. By the 1850s, Becher was one of the busiest lawyers in the region. His clients included the Great Western Railway and Colonel Thomas Talbot. When he died, on July 6, 1885,

Becher owned considerable land, the most valuable property being the 13 acres surrounding "Thornwood," his impressive residence, still standing at 329 St. George Street.

Several notable homes can be found on Becher Street. Built about 1856, "Wincomblea," at number 40, is one of London's few remaining Georgian mansions. Number 49 is an Ontario Cottage, built around 1881, while "Tait Manor," at number 18, is a large Italianate residence, dating from the 1870s.

Dan Brock

Mrs. Sue McDonald and baby Mary Pat in front of the McDonald home on Grosvenor Street in the late 1940s.

BELLWOOD CRESCENT

East. Runs north/south from Watling Street to Falaise Road.

The Bellwood Park subdivision originated in northeast London as a postwar nursery where baby carriages outnumbered cars twenty-to-one. In 1947, street after street of new low-rental homes broke a critical two-year shortage of housing for Second World War veterans and their growing families. Applicants for the 186 neat little bungalows and storey-and-a-half houses were ranked in priority by a Department of Veterans Affairs points system based on length of overseas service and number of children. My family of three (later four) became happy homesteaders at a Grosvenor Street bungalow for $35 a month; the storey-and-a-half houses rented for $45 a month. Our two-bedroom house came equipped with a gas stove and icebox, a wood/coal furnace in the cellar, a back stoop with clothesline pole, seeded lawns in front and back, and a gravel driveway. Our next-door neighbours were ex-Navy and ex-Air Force; I was ex-Army. Besides our shared military backgrounds, many of us were fellow students at The University of Western Ontario, having moved to London to take advantage of the government's program for student veterans.

Today, by virtue of its street names, Bellwood Park remains an ever-green war memorial. Ortona Road, Falaise Road and Apeldoorn Crescent memorialize the battles won by London's Royal Canadian Regiment at Ortona in Italy, by London's First Hussars Armoured Regiment at Normandy's Falaise Gap in France, and by both regiments at Apeldoorn in the liberation of Holland. Watling Street, Wallbrook Crescent, and Mincing Lane pay lasting tribute to some of London, England's most heavily bombed streets. Bellwood Park and its main thoroughfare, Bellwood Crescent, are named after James S. Bell, the city treasurer who played a leading role in the project's financing.

G. Campbell McDonald

BROUGHDALE AVENUE AND BROUGH STREET

North. Broughdale Avenue crosses Richmond Street. Brough Street runs north/south from Huron Street to University Crescent.

Parson (later Archdeacon) Charles Crosbie Brough (1794-1873) left a lasting imprint upon the hamlet of Broughdale. His former rectory, (Brough House, still standing at 1132 Richmond Street), two streets, and the bridge spanning the north branch of the Thames River all owe their names to the Brough family. Born in Ireland, Brough came to Upper Canada in 1832 with his wife, Wilhelmina, and two small daughters, eventually settling in London Township in 1841, where Brough became the incumbent of St. John's Church in Arva. In 1865, Brough built a new rectory on land originally set aside for a clergy reserve on the Proof Line Road (now Richmond Street). Under his ministry, the

Brough's bridge, Richmond Street, below Hellmuth Ladies' College, circa 1870.

parish grew and prospered, and as Archdeacon of London he established new congregations as far north as Goderich.

In 1869, the clergy reserve, minus Brough's rectory and glebe, was surveyed into park lots and put up for sale. Soon the Brough family had neighbours, with names like Turville, Comstock, Berryhill, Murphy, Oke, Hackett, Dickerson and Bernard. They were millers, dairy farmers, carpenters, coopers, barn-builders, poulterers, and businessmen. Broughdale grew slowly and prospered, and today, its community life continues to centre on neighbourliness.

Alex Arthur

BRYDGES STREET

Southeast. Runs east/west between Egerton Street and Wavell Street.

The Great Western Railway, built with British capital, reached London from Hamilton in 1853, and was extended to Windsor the following year. It amalgamated with the Grand Trunk Railway in 1882, and today its track is the Canadian National Railway main line through southern Ontario. In the mid-1860s, several large industries were established in the semi-rural area that became London East. One of these was the Great Western's immense workshop, which was built on land now occupied by the Western Fair's sports facility. The demand for workers' homes prompted the creation of new subdivisions. A nearby development included Brydges Street, which was laid out about 1874 and ran parallel to the railway. Extending north from Brydges were three very short streets, Swinyard, Muir, and Childers, all named for Great Western trustees or senior managers.

Charles John Brydges (1827-89) started his railway career with the London and South-Western Railway in Britain. In 1852, he became managing director of the Great Western Railway. His tenure was tempestuous. By 1862, his relationship with the board had deteriorated and he left to become general manager of the Grand Trunk Railway. Again his performance was mixed, and he resigned in 1874, becoming superintendent of Canadian government railways. That same year, the new president of the Great Western appointed Brydges as a temporary commissioner. When the Conservatives returned to power in 1879, Brydges, a Liberal appointee, was fired and his railway career ended. Later that year, he joined the Hudson's Bay Company as land commissioner. Again he proved to be an effective administrator, but his abrasiveness and aggressiveness caused friction. Brydges died in Winnipeg in 1889.

Christopher Andreae

Richmond Street, looking north towards King Street and the Masonic Temple and Grand Opera House (on the left), in the time of John Brydges.

Richmond Street looking north toward King Street. The former Masonic Temple is on the left.

BURWELL STREET

Central. Runs north/south from Simcoe Street to Dundas Street.

Together with Lt.-Governor Simcoe and Colonel Talbot, Mahlon Burwell was one of London's three founders. He surveyed the site of the city, served in the local government and was a member of the legislature.

Burwell was born in New Jersey in 1783 to a Loyalist family, who immigrated to Upper Canada after the Revolution. In 1810, he married Sarah Haun, with whom he had seven sons, all named after various Classical and British heroes, and two daughters. About the same time, he settled at Port Talbot and became a friend and right-hand man to Colonel Talbot.

Certified in 1809, he surveyed much of what is now southwestern Ontario over the next twenty years and was granted over 40,000 acres in payment for his work. In 1826, he laid out the London town site, following its designation as the district capital. Burwell and Talbot named the streets in honour of leading figures in Britain and the Province of Upper Canada.

During much of this period Burwell was chairman of the magistrates for the London District (which included the counties of Elgin, Norfolk, Middlesex, and Oxford), land registrar for Middlesex, Collector of Customs at Port Talbot, and a school trustee. He was five times elected a Tory member of the provincial legislature. Burwell was also London's first philanthropist. He donated land to the Anglican Church and bequeathed land on Stanley Street for a civic park when he died in 1846.

Frederick H. Armstrong

Robert Carfrae's cottage at 39 Carfrae Street.

CARFRAE STREET AND CRESCENT

Old South. Carfrae Crescent runs north from Grand Avenue to the Thames River; Carfrae Street runs west from Carfrae Crescent to Ridout Street.

In the mid-nineteenth century, Carfrae Street was the road Robert Carfrae took to reach his property, a site overlooking the Thames River in Westminster Township. Carfrae, whose Ontario Cottage is still standing at number 39, was a carpenter from Scotland, who came to London in the late 1820s to work on the new district court-house (today called the Old Court House). He obtained forty acres on the south side of the river and built the present house about 1860. Interestingly, the exterior of the cottage is stuccoed brick, the same technique used at the court-house.

Carfrae Crescent is the principal street in a small subdivision opened in 1908, which turns west near the river to join the older Carfrae Street. The first houses were restricted to the east side of the road because an electric rail line ran down the west side. Known as the Traction Line, the rail line ran from a station on Horton Street, through South London, and on to Port Stanley. It was in service from about 1906 until 1918. Later the rail line's iron bridge was moved a short distance to link Richmond Street to Carfrae Crescent.

Mike Baker

Firemen spraying water into Kingsmill's store on Carling Street during the 1911 fire.

CARLING STREET

Central. Runs east/west from Richmond Street to Talbot Street.

The surname Carling, for many, is synonymous with beer. The Carling Brewery, first located at Waterloo and Pall Mall, was established in 1843 by Thomas Carling. Two sons, William and John, joined the family business and bought it from their father in 1849. Early success allowed them to build a large commercial block on the corner of Richmond and Carling Streets. In later years, the building was the HMCS *Prevost*. The firm outgrew the old brewery in the 1870s and moved to the corner of Talbot and Ann Streets, where a huge new facility was built. It operated until 1936, when Carling was merged with the Kuntz Brewery of Waterloo and the London plant closed.

While William ran the brewery, John ran for office. He won at every level from school trustee and alderman to Parliament — to which he

Sir John Carling upon receiving his knighthood in 1893.

was elected five times. In the 1880s, while a member of John A. Macdonald's cabinet, he brought many things to London, including the infantry school (Wolseley Barracks), the psychiatric hospital (now Regional Mental Health London), and Victoria Park. He was knighted by Queen Victoria in 1893.

Glen Curnoe

CARSON LANE

Central. Runs north/south between Nelson Street and Trafalgar Street.

In October 1904, at the age of 58, William John Carson died while chatting with his physician. Carson was an exemplary educator, and in 1881 was the highest paid teacher in London at $900 per annum. As inspector for the London Board of Education, his particular interests were kindergartens and teacher training. His daughter, Flora, became a kindergarten teacher, and his son, William Oliver, one of London's youngest city councillors. During his ten years as librarian for the

London Public Library, W.O. Carson opened bookshelves to the public, introduced modern reference service, established the Children's Room, launched Story Hour, and opened London's first branch library in the former East London town hall. Relocated to Quebec Street, it was renamed in his honour in 1961. Carson was president of the Ontario Library Association and editor of its *Ontario Library Review*. While inspector of public libraries for the province of Ontario, he established the Ontario Library School in Toronto, making librarianship a recognized profession in the province. Carson's progressive ideas influenced libraries across the province.

Arthur McClelland

CENTRAL AVENUE

Central. Runs east/west from Ontario Street to the Thames River.

Central Avenue is closely identified with the British garrison whose lands it once bisected as Great Market Street. In 1861, the area north of Central became the site of the Provincial Exhibition. The Western Fair was established in 1868 and occupied these grounds until relocating to Queens Park in 1887. The land was then subdivided into building lots.

South of Central, the remaining garrison lands were dedicated as Victoria Park in 1874, five years after the troops had marched away for good. Landscape architect William Miller turned Victoria Park into the 'jewel' of the city, and the nearby building lots became highly desirable. Many of London's elite chose Central Avenue addresses during the 1880s, including lawyer Charles H. Ivey, who lived at number 256, a house later owned by John Labatt. Three successful entrepreneurs — boilermaker Charles W. Leonard, lumberman George Belton, and biscuit king Frank McCormick — made number 284 their address at various times before the First World War.

The rest of Central Avenue remained middle- or working-class over the coming decades. At least one shoemaker and a tinsmith were counted among the scattering of cottage industries further east.

John Mombourquette

Left: 256 Central Avenue, home of some of London's most prominent citizens.

Below: A bird's-eye view of London in 1872 showing the former Imperial Army barracks south of Great Market Street (now Central Avenue).

CHAMBERS AVENUE

North. Runs east/west from Nanette Drive to Sandybrook Drive.

Chambers Avenue makes a long, easy curve from east to west as it rises to the top of Hastings Drive, where the Jack Chambers School is situated. The school was named to honour the late, renowned London artist Jack Chambers, and it is from the school that the avenue derives its name. Chambers trained at H.B. Beal Technical School in the 1940s. After several years of study at the fine art academy in Madrid, he returned to London in 1961 and began painting the southwestern Ontario landscape. He soon developed a reputation as an important young artist and filmmaker.

In 1963, Chambers painted *Summer Behind the House*, a work in which my daughter, Andrea, our golden retriever and myself appear, standing in a field of wild flowers with a row of poplars to the west and a gentle hill rising in the background. In 1988, 10 years after Chambers' tragic death at the age of 47, the London Regional Art Gallery mounted an exhibition of his paintings which included *Summer Behind the House*.

In 1991, when a new school was being built on Hastings Drive, the neighbourhood was asked to submit names for it. One resident, Rosanne Pulford, whose three children would attend the school, visited the site and noticed a row of poplars marking the eastern boundary of the future school yard. Recalling a similar scene in one of the paintings in the Gallery's memorial exhibit, she was inspired to launch her successful campaign to have the school named after Jack Chambers.

Nancy G. Poole

CHAPMAN COURT

Northwest. Runs south from Sarnia Road, west of Wonderland Road.

Chapman Court is a product of the city's program to name streets in honour of servicemen and women, firefighters, and police officers who died in the line of duty. Born in London on March 28, 1926, Kenneth Frank Chapman attended the Wortley Road School and South Collegiate Institute, and was a member of the London South Salvation Army. When he reached the age of service, Chapman enlisted in the Royal Canadian Air Force, earning his air gunner's badge on April 21, 1944. He was posted to 153 Squadron Royal Air Force, and began flying operational raids against targets in occupied Europe in the unit's four-engine Lancaster bombers. Most of his crew were British, the only Canadians being Chapman and Flight Sergeant Cameron Booty from Galt, Ontario. Throughout the fall and into the winter, 153 Squadron attacked targets in the German heartland. They flew under cover of darkness, but casualties were still high. The empty chairs at breakfast following an operation were a sobering reminder that the war in the air was a very dangerous business.

By April 1945, the war in Europe was winding down, but RAF bombers remained active in support of land operations. On April 22, 153 Squadron was assigned to attack the north German port of Bremen, then surrounded by British troops, but the aircraft were called home when it was discovered that the city was obscured by clouds. They were leaving German airspace when a single anti-aircraft gun fired, striking Chapman's Lancaster in the fuselage. The aircraft broke apart in mid-air and the entire seven-man crew was killed. It was Flight Sergeant Chapman's twenty-fourth operation over enemy territory. He had just turned nineteen years of age.

Jonathan Vance

COLONEL TALBOT ROAD

West. Runs north/south between Byron Baseline Road and the Talbot Line (Highway 3) in Elgin County, where it becomes Sunset Road.

Named for Colonel Thomas Talbot (1771-1853), the eccentric, energetic founder of the Talbot Settlement, Colonel Talbot Road is the northern extension of his settlement's road system, which stretched from Long Point to Sandwich (Windsor). Talbot was a younger son of Irish nobleman Richard Talbot. He pursued a career in the British army, serving as aide-de-camp to Lt.-Gov. Simcoe from 1792-94. He accompanied Simcoe to the forks of the Thames and, perhaps inspired by Simcoe's plans for the colony, returned to Upper Canada in 1803 with a land grant on Lake Erie and the authority to settle it.

Eventually, he became the government's land agent for much of what is now southwestern Ontario. As with all of Talbot's roads, lots were laid out on either side and granted to settlers first before a given township's other lots. The settlers did the actual work of opening the roads as one of the conditions for obtaining the deed to a lot. They were also required to clear a portion of their land and build a house. The roads proved to be a key to the success of the settlement, whose population had reached sixty thousand by the time of Talbot's death in 1853.

Douglas Leighton

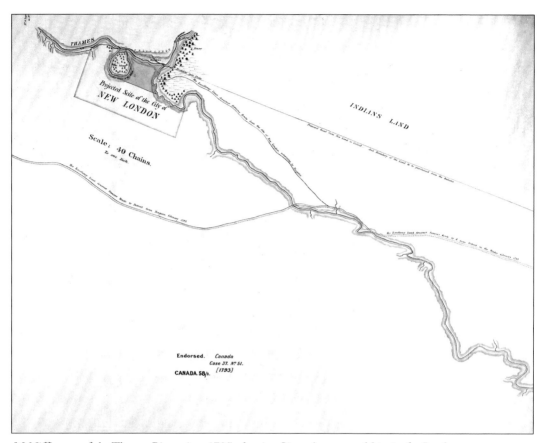

McNiff's map of the Thames River, circa 1795, showing Simcoe's route and his site for London.

COMMISSIONERS ROAD

South. Runs east/west across South London from Hamilton Road to Kilworth.

When John Graves Simcoe journeyed from Niagara to Detroit in 1793, he followed part of a Native trail through the area south of the Thames River. The trail was widened and improved by a government-appointed road commission just prior to the War of 1812 in order to move supplies and troops between Burlington Heights and Detroit. During the war, two skirmishes took place on Reservoir Hill near Springbank Park. On October 6, 1813, the Oxford Militia, which had been escorting a wagon train of wounded soldiers, took a stand on the hill, repelling an advance party of Kentucky riflemen. A second skirmish took place on

August 30, 1814, when the Middlesex Militia ambushed some American troops at the hill.

As early as 1816, farmers with clay deposits on their property established brickyards along Commissioners Road between Wharncliffe and Wonderland Roads. Their portion of the road became known locally as Brick Street, a name retained by Brick Street Cemetery and Brick Street School. The cemetery, in use since 1819, contains many township pioneers — Norton, Topping, Teeple, Stephens, Hall, and Dale — for whom local streets are named. East of Wharncliffe, another stretch of Commissioners became Highland Road after the Highland Golf Club opened in 1922. Fields and woods surrounded the golf course, and the official club history recalls swampy areas that were home to "nasty snapping turtles and maddening mosquitoes."

Glen Curnoe

Brick Street Cemetery.

CORNISH STREET

East. Runs north/south from Brydges Street to Stevenson Avenue.

Francis (Frank) Evans Cornish (1831-78) was both the seventh mayor of London (1861-64) and the first mayor of Winnipeg. He was born in London to Dr. William King Cornish, a man who, at various times, was a lawyer, surgeon, land surveyor, and London village clerk. By the age of twenty-eight, Frank Cornish was a Queen's Counsel and a London alderman.

An Orangeman and a Mason, Cornish was familiar with the rough and tumble style of frontier politics that existed before the advent of the secret ballot. As mayor, he was involved in at least two recorded assaults (against the chief of police and a British army officer), several instances of public drunkenness, a bigamy case, suspected voter fraud, and a well-publicized divorce.

In 1872, Cornish moved to Manitoba, where he became a Crown attorney. He successfully prosecuted Métis leader Ambroise Lepine, one of Louis Riel's senior associates in the Red River Rebellion of 1869-70. Lepine was accused of presiding over the killing of Thomas Scott, a Canadian agitator who openly opposed Riel's short-lived provisional government. Cornish's aggressive prosecution of Lepine made him extremely popular in radical Protestant circles and paved his way to the Mayor's chair in 1874.

John Mombourquette

COVENT MARKET PLACE

Central. Runs from Talbot Street to King Street around the edge of the Market.

Covent Garden Market was named after the original Covent Garden Market in London, England, a twelfth-century kitchen garden that supplied produce to the monks of Westminster Abbey.

In 1840, the board of police in London decided to move the town's central market from its first location on the Court House grounds to a plot east of Wellington. Spurred by the potential loss of a busy market in the commercial centre of town, a group of businessmen donated the land behind their buildings on King and Dundas Streets for a new market. A small structure was built by 1845 and appeared as Covent Garden

Market Lane (now Covent Market Place) looking west towards Talbot Street, circa 1912.

Market on an 1850 map. In 1853, a fine new market was designed by Samuel Peters and a lot purchased for a passageway between the market and the stores on Dundas.

The passage known as Market Lane came to include all the laneways around the market square. To the north, it was home to trust companies, banks, legal offices, wholesale grocers, and produce stands. To the east, it became Temple Street when the Masonic Temple was built on Richmond Street in 1880.

Today, Covent Market Place encircles a new market building, built in

Covent Garden Market, looking northeast from King and Talbot Streets, circa 1910.

2000. Its open, public square is as vibrant as an Italian piazza. There may be more buskers than farmers on some days but our market is surviving with the times.

Ann McColl Lindsay

CRONYN CRESCENT

East. Runs off Cornish Street.

In November 1950, it was announced that Benjamin Cronyn (1840-1905), son of the Anglican bishop of Huron, was among eight mayors whose names would be honoured in a new residential development near Hale and Trafalgar Streets. Before entering politics, Cronyn was a London lawyer, as was his brother Verschoyle, who went on to help found and manage the Huron and Erie Loan and Savings Company (later Canada Trust). Benjamin was first elected mayor in 1874 and returned the following year by acclamation. Although he was a popular mayor, he is perhaps best remembered for a career in finance that was, to say the least, far less distinguished than his brother's. In 1887, it was discovered that he had loaned himself considerable funds from an investment company for which he was solicitor. Unable to pay back the debt, he fled to Vermont, leaving behind his beautiful mansion, "Oakwood," which still stands at 602 Queens Avenue.

Mike Baker

The Benjamin Cronyn House, now 602 Queens Avenue, in the early 1900s.

CRUMLIN ROAD

East. Runs north/south from River Road to London Airport.

Crumlin Road, the former town line for London, West Nissouri, and North Dorchester Townships, was known as Crumlin Sideroad for most of its history. The village of Crumlin was originally called Dreaney's Corners after the blacksmith and hotel owner, Robert Dreaney, an Irishman who settled there in 1846. The hotel, Dreaney House, at Dundas Street, was a stop for the stagecoach from Hamilton to London. In later years, up to 200 teams a day passed through Crumlin, taking farmers and their produce to Covent Garden Market in London.

In 1869, with several commercial enterprises in the area, Dreaney applied to open a post office. In small and far-flung hamlets, post offices not only provided mail service, they also served as meeting places where neighbours could exchange news, discuss local politics, and plan community events. Government officials selected the name "Crumlin" for the crossroads community, which means "winding valley" in Irish. When Highway 2 (now Dundas Street) was widened to a four-lane highway in 1973, many of the businesses at the crossroads were forced to close and Crumlin lost its community identity. With annexation in 1993, Crumlin Sideroad became just Crumlin Road.

Alice Gibb

London's Normal School, circa 1910, now the Monsignor Feeney Centre for Catholic Education at 165 Elmwood Avenue.

DEARNESS DRIVE

South. Runs north/south between Wellington Road and Southdale Road.

Wellington Road was always an important route through Westminster Township. Due to idiosyncrasies in the original surveys, there were two jogs in the road that were eventually eliminated when the automobile replaced the horse as the primary means of transit. One jog led travellers east to today's Dearness Drive. After this road was bypassed in the 1950s by a new section of Wellington Road, it was renamed Dearness Drive for the seniors' residence at its north end. The residence itself was named for educator John Dearness, who was present at its dedication in 1953.

Dearness was born in Hamilton in 1852, and raised on a farm north of London. His lifelong interest in botany developed early. He began teaching in Lucan in 1871, and was appointed inspector of schools for East Middlesex in 1874. He lectured in biology at the Medical School from 1888 until 1914. When London's first teachers' college opened in 1899, he was appointed vice-principal, and then principal in 1918. He is remembered as an "immensely popular teacher."

Dearness wrote extensively on his biological studies and mycology (the study of fungi) collections. He was president of several learned societies including the Mycology Society of America and edited two journals. The John Dearness Public School on Sanatorium Road is named in his honour.

Mike Baker

Gaol and Court House at London, *circa 1843, by George R. Dartnell. This view looks northeast towards Dundas and Ridout Streets.*

DUNDAS STREET

A major central thoroughfare running east/west through London from its eastern boundary to the forks of the Thames.

Dundas Street predates London by more than thirty years. Governor Simcoe intended it to link a future capital of Upper Canada at London with the headwaters of Lake Ontario. For a long time, however, Dundas Street was a road in name only, often impassable to wheeled traffic and merely a trail blazed through the bush at its western end. Sometimes

Above: Dundas Street, south side, looking west towards Richmond Street in the early 1900s.

Left: Dundas Street, north side, looking west from Richmond Street in the mid-1920s.

known as the Governor's Road, Simcoe always intended it to be called Dundas Street to honour Henry Dundas (1742-1811), later Lord Melville, then Secretary of War in the British Cabinet.

Dundas was the last of the great patronage bosses who managed Scotland in the eighteenth century. Righteous in religion and business, the Scots were less so in their politics, making Dundas's job — buying their votes for the government — somewhat easier. He was also the last man to be impeached, in 1806, for malversation of public funds. Although acquitted, he was politically ruined and forced to resign the office he then held as First Lord of the Admiralty.

Fred Dreyer

E A S Y   S T R E E T

South. Runs north/south from Southdale Road ending north of Eden Street.

1945. The Second World War had ended, and soon hundreds of thousands of Canadian soldiers would be returning home. They would be greeted by a generous program of government assistance, better than anything the veterans of the First World War enjoyed, including edu-

Veterans' subdivision, 1946. Southdale Road is in the foreground, and Wellington Road and the Westminster Ponds are toward the right.

cational credits, job training, business start-up funds, and housing. Across the country, the Department of Veterans Affairs began to build subdivisions full of small but modern homes to accommodate Canada's veterans. The Southdale subdivision was part of this program, and in 1947 the government announced that its streets would be named after the great leaders of the Allied war effort: Churchill, McArthur, Eden, Roosevelt, and Montgomery. But the residents of the new subdivision had other ideas. What self-respecting veteran wanted to live on a street named after a general, even a successful one? So they picked their own names. Creston replaced Roosevelt; Verulam replaced McArthur; and Winblest replaced Churchill. And in the most inspired choice of all, Montgomery was re-christened Easy Street. One of the residents had remarked that life in Southdale was like living on Easy Street, and the name stuck with the locals. Soon, there was a plywood street sign on the corner; for a time it was even topped by an old rocking chair.

But the changes did not sit well with the Township of Westminster, which refused to recognize the new names, or with the city of London, which annexed the area in 1961. The residents persisted and petitioned the city to accept the names that had been in general use for more than a decade. On December 7, 1964, Judge Ian MacRae heard the petition and decreed that the names of the generals and statesmen would be dropped. At last the residents of Southdale were truly living on Easy Street.

Jonathan Vance

EULA WHITE PLACE

Southeast. Runs east from Deveron Crescent, east of Pond Mills Road.

Eula White, OBE, was born, lived, and died in London, Ontario (1894-1985). She was the granddaughter of George White, who came to London in 1857 and founded an implement company that made thresh-ing machines and portable steam engines. White lived with her family on Euclid Avenue and attended Wortley Road School; later she attended private school in Toronto. While her friends were content with playing bridge and golf, White was determined to make London a better community.

In January 1946, *The London Free Press* reported: "The woman-a-block plan, operated under the Central Volunteer Bureau, has had Miss White's leadership since its inception several years ago, and she still heads the executive body of this 1000 woman organization by means of

The Active Service Club during the Second World War.

which many city-wide chores have been accomplished with much effi-ciency and little fuss." This last phrase describes perfectly the way Eula White did so many things.

She was a leading member of the Imperial Order Daughters of the Empire (IODE) for nearly thirty years and served on the city's Mother's Allowance Board and later on the board of the YMCA/YWCA. It was for her wartime activities, however, that White won the hearts of Londoners and the Order of the British Empire (OBE). From 1940-45, Eula ran the Active Service Club in the old "Y," the former library at the southwest corner of Wellington Street and Queens Avenue. The club provided food, lodging, and recreation for every serviceman who walked through its doors. It was a tremendous undertaking and White managed it magnificently.

In her later years, Eula lived with her sister Shirley at Ballybrack Farm, a charming cottage just east of Pond Mills Road, where they tended their pear orchard and delivered fruit each autumn to Covent Garden Market. The farm was just north of Eula White Crescent and Eula White Place.

Nancy Poole

FERGUSON PLACE

South. Runs east/west from Ridout Street to Bellevue Avenue.

James Ferguson came to Canada in 1824 as a young man. After farming with his father, he became a road builder, securing contracts for several roads including Egremont Road from London to Sarnia. In 1850, he helped construct the main line of the Great Western Railway.

By then Ferguson was a prominent London citizen and was appointed Registrar for Middlesex County following an election defeat. He established his magnificent estate on Grand Avenue near Ridout as early as the 1850s. "The Beeches" was one of several substantial Grand Avenue properties that solidified South London's reputation as a wealthy residential neighbourhood.

The drawing of Ferguson's estate in the 1878 *Atlas of Middlesex County* shows a two-storey, Regency-style mansion surrounded by a topiary garden of trees and bushes. An ornamental gateway leads to a circular lane that crosses a meandering stream. Cows graze peacefully in the bucolic distance.

The executors of Ferguson's estate subdivided the property in 1887. Over the next few decades, as surrounding streets were developed, Ferguson Place remained a field. "The Beeches" survived a string of owners until, in ramshackle condition, it was demolished in 1959 for a high-rise apartment building.

John H. Lutman

"The Beeches" from the 1878 Historical Atlas of Middlesex County.

FORD CRESCENT

Northwest. Runs between Neville Drive and Coombs Avenue.

Arthur Rutherford Ford (1880-1968) was best known as editor-in-chief and later editor-emeritus of *The London Free Press* during his sixty-year career in journalism. He founded The University of Western Ontario's School of Journalism in 1945, and became chancellor of the University (1947-1955) after serving nineteen years as a member of its board of governors.

Ford travelled widely as a journalist and attended the first meeting of the United Nations in San Francisco in 1945. He was active in public affairs and for many years had a keen interest in the battle against cancer. He was a member of the Royal Commission established in 1931 by the Province of Ontario that visited the United States, England, France, Belgium, Germany, and Sweden to investigate means of fighting the disease. The recommendations of the Commission were largely implemented during Ford's term as chairman of the Ontario Cancer Research and Treatment Foundation, a position he held from its inception in 1944 until 1953.

Arthur Ford was a trusted confidant to several prime ministers, including Sir Robert Borden, Sir Wilfrid Laurier, Arthur Meighen, R.B. Bennett, and William Lyon Mackenzie King. Arthur Ford Public School, at 417 Viscount Road, is named in his honour.

Jim Etherington

FOX AVENUE

Northwest. Runs north/south between Tamblyn Drive and Trott Drive.

After being coaxed to what was then called The Western University of London, Ontario from Princeton in 1917, Classics professor Dr. W. Sherwood Fox (1878-1967) told his new employers that he could not possibly consider an administrative post, stating: "It is quite clear to me that I am naturally unfitted for a life of that kind." Within two years he was the university's dean of arts, and within a decade, its president (1928-47). Despite a difficult beginning as president — his inauguration was postponed due to what he described as a nervous breakdown — Fox guided Western through a period of impressive growth, from seven hundred full-time students to 2500, and physical expansion.

University College at The University of Western Ontario.

London has Fox to thank for much of Western's present-day beauty. In the mid-1930s, he had twelve thousand trees planted on campus, ensuring that every tree species in Western Ontario was represented. The title of his column in *The London Free Press*, "By Hook and Book," demonstrated his combined interests in scholarship and nature. Fox is probably best remembered internationally for writing: "Are all fishermen liars? Or do only liars fish?"

London pushed west and north after the Second World War, in tandem with Western's own expansion. The new University Heights subdivision honoured Western *prominenti*, and Fox was one of them.

Alan MacEachern

Frank Place.

FRANK PLACE

Old South. Connects Windsor Crescent and Wellington Road.

Richard Frank, a native of Yorkshire, England, came to London to work as a joiner. In 1843, he was both councillor and pathmaster for St. Andrew's Ward. In 1845, he purchased three hundred acres bordering Wellington Road, a few miles south of London in Westminster Township, and began farming. Frank also owned a sawmill and brick-yard on the banks of the Thames River, southeast of Clark's Bridge, which links Wellington Street and Wellington Road. He ran the sawmill for more than a quarter of a century.

Frank served on the Westminster Township Council from 1850-54, holding the position of deputy reeve in 1850 and reeve in 1851. About 1862, his family moved into the two-storey Georgian-style brick home that is now 1 Frank Place. It became a part of the Foxbar subdivision — the first in London with curved streets — when the subdivision was laid out by surveyor F.W. Farncomb in 1921. The house has belonged to Redeemer Lutheran Church since 1957, and has been physically linked to the church.

Dan Brock

FRANKLIN AVENUE

South. Runs east/west between Ridout Street and Wortley Road.

Four generations of Flecksers have lived on this beautiful Old South street. My grandfather, John Franklin (Frank) Fleckser, moved from Hamilton with his wife, Christina, and their four children and bought land on London's southern edge in the 1920s. They lived in a solid brick cottage on the property and Frank, an engineer, worked at McClary's stove company.

The children attended Wortley Road Public School and played in a meadow with three tall pine trees, an apple orchard, and a creek that overflowed every spring. During the Depression, Frank subdivided the land into building lots, naming its street Franklin. The city suggested "Fleckser Park," but the shy gentleman farmer gave a resounding "no" to the idea.

My father, Harold, and his sister Ruth sold some of their lots, and Roy James, a renowned contractor, built many new homes. Beyond the new backyards was Westminster Township, fields of clover, a herd of friendly cows, and gravel roads.

Franklin Avenue became a street of closely linked families. At one time more than thirty children lived there. Every winter, fathers made a neighbourhood skating rink and every summer, families would holiday together.

Don Fleckser

Franklin Fleckser (front row, centre) and his family.

The back yards of houses on Front Street during the flood of 1947.

FRONT STREET

South. Runs off Wellington Road south of Clark's Bridge.

In 1937, nearly fifty families lived on this street. Their frame cottages had been built on low-lying land fronting the Thames River, and after spring break-up, children played on large chunks of ice that washed into backyards, while parents cursed soggy basements. More than seasonal inconveniences, these were signs that their land belonged to the river.

During the last weekend of April, 1937, a torrential rain fell, soaking the earth so that there was almost total runoff into the river. By noon on Monday, April 27, water filled Front Street. As the river rose and the current strengthened, gas and water connections were severed. Large craters appeared in the earth. Concrete slabs were wrenched out of the sidewalk. The Butson home was lifted off its foundation, carried downstream, and dashed to pieces on Clark's Bridge. The couple's terrier perished in the wreckage.

Front Street never recovered; it faded away, one home at a time. The city offered to exchange lots on other streets for a dollar so the remaining houses could be re-located, but homeowners had to cover moving expenses. Subsequent floods in 1947 and 1948 prompted the conversion of the street into parkland. Today, only a street sign and incongruous manhole covers on the bike path hint that the area was once a residential street.

Christopher Doty

GAMMAGE STREET

East. Runs north/south between Oxford Street and Victoria Street.

James Gammage (1808-91) was one of Canada's first florists. Born in Whitney, England, he attended Oxford University and worked in the woollen industry before immigrating to London. By 1869, he had established his florist business, which prospered and expanded. He acquired twenty-three acres on Oxford Street, east of Adelaide Street, where, by 1886, Gammage could boast of having the largest greenhouses west of Montreal. After his death, his sons, William Wallace and James Gardiner, carried on the business. James Gardiner also opened Gard Gammage Flowers in Hotel London in 1936, relocating in 1961 to 235 Dundas Street. William Wallace established the Gardeners' and Florists' Association of Canada and was the first Canadian member of the Florists' Telegraph Delivery Association. In the spring of 1971, Gammage sold out to John McKerlie and retired after forty-three years in the family business. But flowers were in his blood, and he still operated a flower gift shop in Bayfield afterwards. McKerlie relocated to 747 Waterloo Street at Oxford Street in June 1982, and sold Gammage Flowers to John and Sarah Geddes in 1996.

Arthur McClelland

An advertisement for Gammage's showing the greenhouses on Oxford Street, 1900.

GEARY AVENUE

North. Runs north/south between Fanshawe Park Road and Stoney brook Crescent.

William and Elizabeth (Jones) Geary and their five children emigrated from Ireland in 1818, becoming part of London Township's first group of settlers. William was assigned the northern half of Lot 14, Concession 5, and his older son, John, the southern half. Two hundred fifty people gathered in William's barn in 1822 for the first Anglican services in the township, the beginning of St. John the Divine Church, Arva.

   John and Eliza (Haskett) had two sons who owned approximately 450 acres in Concessions 4 and 5. Robert owned one farm, but John Jr. was the major landowner. A lawyer, oil refiner, and a co-founder of Imperial Oil in 1880, he built a palatial home, "Bli Bro," near the northwest corner of Fanshawe Road and Adelaide Street. This intersection was known as Geary Corners. North of his house he built the Geary Cheese Factory, which operated until 1901. The last of the family property was sold in the 1920s. Bli Bro has been torn down, but two former Geary residences remain on the north side of Fanshawe, a large brick house opposite Geary Avenue and another farther west.

Catherine B. McEwen

GIBBONS PLACE

North. A cul-de-sac off Talbot Street, overlooking Gibbons Park.

Gibbons Place and Park honour Sir George Christie Gibbons. He was born in St. Catharines, attended Upper Canada College, and became a successful lawyer, businessman, and defining figure among London's elite. He built "Lornehurst," a grand residence overlooking Victoria Park. Gibbons founded the London and Western Trusts Company Limited in 1896, served as president of the City Gas Company, and was a director of the London Life Insurance Company. A founder of both the London Club and the London Hunt Club, he served on the original 1908 board of governors of what was then called The Western University of London, Ontario.

   A staunch Liberal and confidant of Prime Minister Sir Wilfrid Laurier, Gibbons was appointed in 1905 to the Canadian section of the

International Waterways Commission, a body formed to investigate issues relating to Canada-United States boundary waters. He became the Canadian negotiator in the complex, bruising discussions that produced the International Boundary Waters Treaty of 1909. Gibbons promoted the creation of a permanent body to settle differences between the two countries according to agreed-upon principles. Only in this way, he reasoned, would Canada be treated fairly. Accordingly, the treaty provided for the International Joint Commission, which still functions, and specified that both countries were to have "equal and similar rights" in the use of boundary waters. His work is remembered in a plaque in Gibbons Park erected by the Historic Sites and Monuments Board of Canada.

The Gibbons family gave the park to London in 1927 in memory of Sir George. The land was purchased from Catherine Becher, who lived at "Thornwood," the charming nineteenth-century mansion overlooking the park.

Peter Neary

GRAND AVENUE

South. Runs east/west from Ridout Street, crossing Wellington Road.

The 1893 Bird's Eye View of London shows just how grand Grand Avenue was. Here London's lords of industry created their versions of

Waverley, at left, and Grand Avenue looking east from Ridout Street, circa 1910.

Waverley in the early 1900s.

British country estates, with turreted and multi-gabled mansions sur-rounded by extensive grounds. Six were of special note. "The Beeches" was a late Georgian residence, built in the 1850s for County Registrar James Ferguson. Further east was the ostentatious home of biscuit-maker Andrew McCormick, a four-storey tower dominating its broad front façade. Towards High Street on the hillside, the more restrained "Parkwood" was built for an Imperial Oil Company co-founder, J.R. Minhinnick. Grand Avenue also boasted "Waverley," a Queen Anne showplace designed for Charles Goodhue, son of London millionaire George J. Goodhue, and expanded by T.H. Smallman, another Imperial Oil founder. Next was "Woodlands," the large Italianate home of wholesale grocer Charles Richardson; and then "Idlewyld," another pic-turesque Queen Anne mansion, built by Charles Hyman, Minister of Public Works in Sir Wilfrid Laurier's cabinet, who often entertained the prime minister there.

Today, only Waverley and Idlewyld remain. The broad parks once surrounding the houses are gone, but many of their luxurious architec-tural features have been retained or restored.

Nancy Tausky

HALE STREET

East. Runs north/south between Hamilton Road and Dundas Street.

William Hale (1804-64) moved from York (Toronto) to London to manufacture bricks for the new district court-house in the late 1820s. During the Rebellion of 1837, he was among the Reformers who met at Flannagan's Tavern on December 8 to decide how to support Mackenzie's uprising locally. The Reformers were rounded up by the militia and confined to the jailhouse Hale had helped to build. When his case came before the Grand Jury, Hale was acquitted of the charge of treason. Later in life, he recounted the story of how the prison guards, occupying the room below the prisoners, amused themselves by firing bullets through the ceiling. Undaunted by his brush with the law, William Hale remained active in Reform politics. On an 1878 township map, Hale Street is shown running through the family's land, much of which has been subdivided into smaller lots.

Arthur McClelland

HALL'S MILLS ROAD

Byron. Runs north/south from Commissioners Road West toward the Thames River.

Hall's Mills was an early name for Byron, a post office hamlet in the former Westminster Township. In the 1830s, Burleigh Hunt built a dam, gristmill, and a carding and fulling mill on the banks of the Thames. He took Cyrenius Hall into partnership, and sold him the business in 1836. Hall was born in New Hampshire, and contracted in Upper Canada for the British forces in the War of 1812. After acquiring these Westminster mills, he added a distillery and tannery, and brought his three sons into his diversified business. In the 1851 census, Hall

The millstone behind the Byron branch of the London Public Library.

An old driveshed on Hall's Mills Road.

reported he had produced 2000 yards of cloth, employed seven hands in the cloth manufactory, and finished two thousand hides at the tannery. The mill attached to the distillery could thrash fifteen to twenty bushels of grain at once when in good repair.

The mills had many more owners, including the Ross Brothers, who added a steam-powered sawmill. The sawmill ruins disappeared in the flood of 1937. A millstone behind the Byron Branch of the London Public Library bears a historic plaque commemorating Hall's pioneer industries.

Hilary Bates Neary

HAMILTON ROAD

Southeast. Runs from Bathurst Street and Burwell Street east toward Dorchester.

Hamilton Road was first surveyed in the 1830s, and White's Bridge, which linked London and Westminster Townships, was built over the south branch of the Thames River in 1833. Hamilton Hartley Killaly (*see* **KILALLY ROAD**) improved the road as commissioner of public works. Named not for him, but rather its destination, Hamilton Road was bridged, graded, gravelled, and planked through the pine forest to Dorchester. When British troops marched out of London in 1854 for service in the Crimean War, the proprietor of the White Ox Inn at 495 Hamilton Road served refreshments to cheer them on their way. Known as "the Brantford Road" beyond the city, it earned Middlesex County income from tolls. By the 1920s, the London Street Railway provided streetcar service to Ealing Street in stiff competition with the private Metropolitan Bus Company. London refused to renew private licences when Metropolitan left in 1926, prompting Hamilton Road residents to march to Mayor John Moore's house on Waterloo Street in protest. To East Londoners, proud of their vibrant community, Hamilton Road is popularly known as "the Ham."

Arthur McClelland

HAZELDEN LANE

West. Runs east/west between Hyde Park Road and Hartson Road.

Many city streets recognize people or families, but Hazelden Lane honours a house. "Hazelden" (now 1132 St. Anthony Road) was the

The south side of Hazelden, circa 1910.

J. W. Little, 1900.

gracious summer-house of the Little family, surrounded by hazelnut trees, and overlooking the Thames. Generations of Littles contributed significantly to London and its university. Lieutenant Colonel J.W. Little founded Robinson, Little & Co. dry goods wholesalers, served as mayor, and promoted the development of Springbank Park.

Established in 1878 by the Anglican Church, The Western University of London, Ontario as it was then called, was in financial difficulties by 1906. Little joined a blue-ribbon committee that considered options for maintaining the university's viability. Their recommendations were accepted, and in 1908 the university became non-denominational and supported by the city with $5,000 annually for five years. Little was elected vice-chairman of Western's board of governors, and held that position until his death in 1913.

Arthur Little succeeded his father on the board, and was its chair from 1919 to 1954. During 35 years of service, he oversaw Western's extraordinary growth and development. His name appeared on the purchase agreement when the university acquired its present site, and he presided at the ground breaking for its first buildings.

The former J.W. Little Memorial Stadium was built by the legacy of Colonel Little's widow in 1929. The J.W. Little Pavilion at the new TD Waterhouse Stadium honours his memory.

Jim Etherington

HELLMUTH AVENUE

North. Runs north/south from Oxford Street to Grosvenor Street.

Hellmuth Avenue is named for Isaac Hellmuth (1817-1901), the second bishop of the Anglican Diocese of Huron, first principal of Huron University College and founder of what was then called The Western University of London, Ontario. The avenue bisects the site of Hellmuth Boys' College (1864-77), which occupied the block bounded by Wellington, Grosvenor, Waterloo, and St. James Streets.

Energetic and entrepreneurial, Isaac Hellmuth came to London in 1862 at Bishop Benjamin Cronyn's invitation to assist with establishing what it now known as Huron University College. At the same time, he built a private school for boys (1864) and one for girls (1869). Hellmuth Ladies' College (1869-99) was located on the site of today's Mount St. Joseph Motherhouse on Richmond Street North. The depression of the 1870s contributed to the Hellmuth Boys' College's demise, and in 1878, the school became Dufferin College, Western's first home. Vacant by the middle 1880s, the building was used for a time as a tile warehouse and demolished about 1894. Subdivision of the property had begun: as early as November 1888, the Church of St. John the Evangelist had opened at the southwest corner of the block. The middle of the site was developed residentially in the latter 1890s.

The houses here, constructed a century and more ago, give the street an Edwardian flavour.

Douglas Leighton

St. James Street looking west from Hellmuth Avenue toward the Church of St. John the Evangelist, circa 1910.

HOPE STREET

Central. A cul-de-sac running west from Colborne Street.

Brothers Adam and Charles J. Hope were London merchants and members of the United Presbyterian Church. Their street was once a lane leading to the church cemetery, located at the southwest corner of Princess and Colborne Streets. In 1852, the town council passed a bylaw forbidding burials within the town limits. The church trustees had the property surveyed and divided into building lots and placed an advertisement in what is now *The London Free Press* requesting "persons having friends buried in the late Cemetery … to remove them within two weeks." The graves were probably moved to the Presbyterian Cemetery on Oxford Street West.

Adam emigrated from Scotland in 1834, moving to London in 1845 to join John Birrell in a hardware, dry goods, and grocery business. He left the partnership in 1851, opening Adam Hope & Co., general wholesale merchants, importing British, French, German, and American dry goods, groceries, and hardware. He was the first president of the London Board of Trade (later the Chamber of Commerce) of which he and Charles were charter members, and a founder in 1864 of the Huron and Erie Loan and Savings Company (later Canada Trust). The Hope brothers moved to Hamilton in 1865, where Adam relocated the retail hardware department of his former business.

Glen Curnoe

HORTON STREET

Central. Runs east/west from Adelaide Street, originally only to Thames Street, later extended to Springbank Drive.

Sir Robert John Wilmot Horton (1784-1841) was British Under Secretary of State for War and the Colonies from 1821-28. Colonel Thomas Talbot had met Wilmot (the surname Horton was added in 1832 for family reasons) in the "other London" in 1822 during negotiations with British officials about Talbot's settlement in Upper Canada. Wilmot had impressed Talbot with his knowledge about planned emigration and his professionalism and courtesy. Wilmot viewed colonial settlement as a solution to problems of overpopulation and poverty and encouraged settlement schemes such as Talbot's. These views were eventually dismissed as expensive and counter-productive, as many "planned" immigrants arriving in Upper Canada soon left for the United States.

Horton Street provided a connection to Hamilton Road for Londoners travelling east in the period before the railway era. Its modern extension westward across the Thames River to Springbank Drive in the 1980s was controversial because of the necessary demolition of houses on the north side of Beaconsfield Avenue. Largely commercial, the street today is the location of the Central Fire Hall, Labatt's Brewery, and the Salvation Army's Men's Mission.

Douglas Leighton

HUBREY ROAD

South. Runs north/south from Enterprise Drive to Green Valley Road.

Hubrey Road is named after a hamlet that developed near what is now the intersection of Highbury Avenue South and Westminster Drive. The village consisted of the First Free Church, Jock Cochrane's tavern, Hubrey Post Office, and Hubrey School.

Originally the hamlet was called "The Hub," a name thought to have originated from a lecture given at the school by Premier George W. Ross, in which he described the corner as the "hub of Ontario." More likely, the name is the result of the village's location near the centre, or hub, of the township. In 1890, a post office was applied for to be called The Hub. Officials decided this name would not do because there was already in existence "The Hub of New York." The name "Hubrey" was given instead, probably because of its similarity to the word Hub.

Hubrey School was best known for one outstanding teacher, Flora McColl, who taught from 1875-80 and 1889-1904. In 1879, she had 79 pupils of all ages in her one-room school. In 1893, her class won the bronze medal for freehand drawing and penmanship at the World's Columbia Exposition in Chicago. This school, one of Hubrey's last buildings, closed in 1965. Today, the surviving part of it houses the Croatian Sports Centre.

Jennifer Grainger

Hyatt Avenue.

HYATT AVENUE

East. Runs north/south from Little Grey Street to Little Hill Street.

The Hyatt Brothers, a general contracting and building business, was founded in London in 1896 by George R. and John F. Hyatt. In 1897, two other brothers, Albert E. and Henry T., joined the firm.

 The Hyatt Brothers built all but two of the houses on Hyatt Avenue. By August 1905, the first eleven brick houses were completed on the east side of the street. The houses on the west side followed, the first being the home of George R. Hyatt. They also built the Hyatt Avenue Methodist (now United) Church at the south end of the street facing Hamilton Road in 1907-08.

 Present-day structures built by the firm include the Egerton Street Baptist Church, Calvary United Church, St. Andrew Memorial Anglican Church, Trafalgar Street School, the Palace Theatre, and the former City Hall on the northeast corner of Dundas and Wellington Streets. The workmanship and pride of the company is evident in the houses they built on Sycamore Street, Elm Street, Rosewood Avenue, Baker Street, Windsor Avenue, and Ridout Street.

Glen Curnoe

HYMAN STREET

Charles Hyman in the mid-1890s.

Central. Runs east/west from St. George Street to Waterloo Street.

Between the late 1830s and the 1870s, London grew from an administrative town into the economic centre of Upper Canada, thanks to the efforts of a small group of local entrepreneurs. These men first developed specialized mercantile and manufacturing businesses, gradually expanded their operations beyond the city, and then established the major financial institutions that made London a metropolitan centre.

Among these entrepreneurial leaders was Ellis Walton Hyman, who was born in Pennsylvania in 1813. Trained as a tanner, he came to London in 1834 and began supplying leather goods to the British garrison. His tannery business grew and, in the 1870s, he started a shoe factory with his son, Charles. They opened branches throughout southwestern Ontario.

Hyman helped to incorporate the Board of Trade in 1857, the Huron and Erie Savings and Loan Company (later Canada Trust) in 1864, and the London Life Insurance Company in 1874. He built London's first music hall in 1866 at the corner of Richmond and York Streets. By the time he died in 1878, Hyman was worth some $250,000 and employed seventy-five men. Charles, London's Member of Parliament in the early 1900s, continued the business, which included a large tannery on Richmond Street, near Mill Street, which operated into the 1960s. Hyman Street, two blocks south of the Richmond Street tannery site, is all that remains of the family's political and industrial legacy.

Frederick H. Armstrong

JALNA BOULEVARD

South. Circles the White Oaks Subdivision.

In 1971, the CBC broadcasted a dramatization of Mazo de la Roche's saga of the Whiteoak family and their home, Jalna. At that time, the developers of the White Oaks Subdivision — one of London's largest, with homes for thirty thousand people — were searching for street names.

The proximity of White Oak Sideroad made a connection with the series irresistible, and one of the city's planners entrusted a friend who was reading the novels to note names for possible use in the subdivision. Thus characters from the Canadian classic came to live in South

White Oaks Mall and Wellington Road during the early 1970s.

London. There weren't enough names in the book for all the streets, however, so references to more recent popular culture, such as Ponderosa Crescent, were also used.

Denis Hammond

JARVIS STREET

Southwest. Runs north/south off Springbank Drive.

Several Jarvis families arrived in Westminster Township in the early years of the nineteenth century. By the 1820s, they were settled on lots, located largely in Concession 1 and the Broken Front Concession along the Thames River. They were all farmers except Eli Samuel, who was an accomplished brick-maker. The progeny of this clan contributed to their growing community and found success farther afield. Chauncey Giles Jarvis, born in 1860 to Eli Samuel Jarvis, was a prominent lawyer in the London area and a founder of the Baconian Club in 1884. Dr. Chester Jarvis, born in 1876 to Lyman Jarvis, became Director of

Agricultural Training in the United States Bureau of Education in Washington, D.C. Nicholas Jarvis, born in 1832, was a popular teacher at the old Brick Street School on Commissioners Road for thirty-six years before he retired in 1887. He was remembered for his impeccable grooming and exquisite penmanship.

Anne McKillop

JIM ASHTON STREET

East. Runs north/south between Oxford Street and Mardell Street.

A London labour organizer with a lifelong love of the drums was honoured with a street named for him near the Canadian Auto Workers (CAW) hall where he did some of his most important work. Jim Ashton died of a heart attack on October 25, 1994, at age forty-six, just over a week after being named a national representative in the CAW regional office in London. He was in his fourth term as president of the London and District Labour Council, which he had headed since 1988, and had just completed nine years as president of CAW Local 27, one of the largest locals in the union.

Al Seymour, area director of the CAW, said of Ashton's involvement in fostering London's labour movement: "He helped build coalitions to oppose things like free trade. He was a demonstrator for the working class." Ashton had been organizing London plants since the early 1970s. The city council's decision to rename Seven-Up Avenue in his memory drew support from the twenty-thousand member labour council and many other citizens. The bylaw took effect September 4, 1995.

Ashton brought the same passion to drumming as he did to labour activities. As a student in the 1960s, he was the drummer for a Belmont rock band called the Village Guild. It was a longhaired outfit; Ashton and his band mates loved the Rolling Stones. But the Canadian music industry at that time was a tough place to make a living, so Ashton decided to leave the band and study psychology at Waterloo Lutheran University (now Wilfrid Laurier University). His friends in the London labour community would say he made the right decision.

Jim Ashton often took up his sticks to play the drums when he had the chance. In his life and work, the beat always went on.

James Reaney

KAINS ROAD

West. RiverBend. Once ran from Commissioners Road to the Kains farm; now runs from the Oxford Street extension into RiverBend.

Archibald Kains was born in Quebec in 1825. After farming near Exeter, running a distillery with his brother in St. Thomas, and searching as far away as Texas for a property suitable for a cattle ranch, he finally settled on land in the northwest corner of Westminster Township in 1863. Kains acquired a four-hundred-acre farm, naming it River Bow Farm. His greatest accomplishment, in his view, was the building of a herd of Ayreshire cattle from a single heifer calf.

Following Kains' death at age sixty, each of his four sons inherited a part of the farm. The RiverBend area had once been a tight-knit farming community that included families such as the Shores, the Kilbourns, the Cassadys, and the Bainards, most of whom had dispersed by the time urban development arrived in the late 1990s.

Kains Road itself was to have disappeared until the developer, Sifton Properties, convinced the City to retain part of it. It now runs north from Oxford Street in almost the same location as when Archie Kains lived at the end of it.

Mike Baker

KELLOGG'S LANE

East. Runs north/south between Dundas Street and Florence Street.

Baby and breakfast cereal — the "health foods" of their time — were first developed by doctors to provide better nutrition for patients. John Kellogg, an American scientist, was determined to create a "wholesome, nourishing, and palatable" breakfast cereal. Two doctors inspired by Kellogg established the Battle Creek Sanitarium Health Food Company in London at 649-651 Colborne Street in 1898. It was managed by Thomas H. Robinson, proprietor of the Robinson Corset Company. The enterprise was not a financial success, but the concept attracted some London businessmen, who bought the assets, paid Kellogg $75,000 for the Canadian rights, and began manufacturing corn-flakes. In 1915, the company built a new factory on Dundas Street, using hydro power to run machinery and steam for cooking. Meanwhile, Kellogg's brother Will had established a Toronto branch making the identical product in almost identical packaging. The two companies fought a legal battle to establish sole rights to the Corn Flakes™ monopoly. The dispute was settled in 1923, with Will Kellogg buying out the London operation. The following year, the Toronto plant closed and Kellogg's enlarged the Dundas Street plant, adding automatic machinery and new products, including Bran Flakes™, All Bran™, and Rice Krispies™.

Hilary Bates Neary

KILALLY ROAD

Northeast. Runs east/west from below Fanshawe Dam to Edgevalley Road.

Hamilton Hartley Killaly was born in Dublin in 1800, where he became an engineer after graduating from Trinity College. He and his wife Martha immigrated to Canada in 1835, settling on a four-hundred-acre piece of land on Concession 4 near present-day Kilally Road. The spelling of the street name differs somewhat from the spelling of his name.

Killaly built a three-storey timber frame house he called Killaly Castle on a bluff overlooking the river. He farmed there until he obtained a position with the Welland Canal Company. Following the union of the Canadas in 1841, he was elected London's Parliamentary representative and then appointed commissioner of public works. While in office, Killaly improved the area's major roads greatly by planking, graveling, and grading those leading into the city from the nearest ports including Hamilton, Sarnia, Port Stanley, and Windsor.

Though he left the area in the 1850s, his former lands continued to be called Killaly Flats. Tradition has it that Fanshawe Road was named after a village in Ireland where Killaly once lived.

Dan Brock

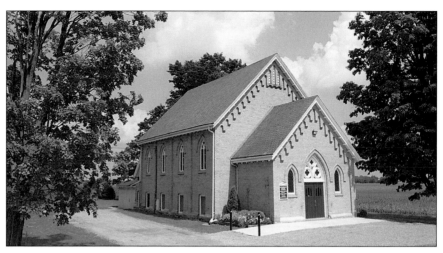

Littlewood United Church.

LITTLEWOOD DRIVE

Southwest. Runs east/west from the city limits to Wonderland Road South.

In the 1800s, the hamlet of Littlewood could be found at the former Westminster and Delaware town lines, now the intersection of Littlewood Drive and Westdel Bourne. Some original buildings survive, including the school, which was built in 1879 and is now a private home. At the end of Littlewood Drive is a house where the first post office opened in 1885. The building to the right, once a general store, was previously the second post office.

"Littlewood" is English, but its local provenance is uncertain. One version has Thomas Weekes, a settler from Devon, who purchased land on the west side of the town line, naming the community after his birthplace.

A Methodist church was constructed on the east side of the town line, but by the 1890s the congregation had outgrown it and decided to build anew. As workmen began tearing down the building, they learned that a young couple, Frank Dores and Jenny Weekes, were planning to get married that day. Work stopped immediately: the couple married at 10:00 A.M. and the church was demolished by 3:00 P.M. The new building — now Littlewood United Church — is still used for services today.

Jennifer Grainger

LOMBARDO AVENUE

North. Runs north/south between Regent and Victoria Streets.

Although he had been a professional musician in his hometown of London, Ontario since 1918, band-leader Guy Lombardo's show business career officially took off in 1924 — the year his band, The Royal Canadians, permanently settled in the United States.

The fall of 1949 marked the 25th anniversary of this milestone. Lombardo's record company, Decca, released a special commemorative album, and on September 16, Lombardo arrived at the NBC Studios in New York City for what he believed was a routine radio interview. Instead he found a studio audience, an orchestra, and host Ralph Edwards of the biography program "This Is Your Life." For the next half-hour, Lombardo's life was touchingly recreated with anecdotes from family members, colleagues, and childhood friends. As a result of the program, London's city council named a new residential street after the band-leader in a north-end neighbourhood.

In a career spanning more than fifty years, The Royal Canadians sold over 100 million records — more than any other big band — and topped the charts twenty-one times.

Christopher Doty

Lebert, Carmen, and Guy Lombardo on Lombardo Avenue, 1950.

MASONVILLE CRESCENT AND COURT

North. Runs south from Sunnyside Drive.

Crossroads encourage taverns. Peter McMartin opened one in 1850 at the corner of the Proof Line Road (later Richmond Street) and the fifth Concession (present-day Fanshawe Park Road). A hamlet grew there, which became known as McMartin's Corners. Travellers heading north to Goderich or west to Sarnia, and farmers with produce for London's market, refreshed themselves and their horses at McMartin's hotel. Robert Mason, an Irish settler, opened another hotel there in 1858. A reliable fellow, he was commissioned postmaster in 1874 and opened a post office in the Mason House. The crossroads were now called Masonville. Small manufactories were established, including the Bryan Brush and Broom Factory, Hewings' boot and shoe factory, and Heighway's wagon and carpentry shop. Masonville had a blacksmith's shop, dressmaker, grocers, veterinarian, and even a fishmonger, who sold fresh catches from Grand Bend. After the arrival of the automobile, the crossroads were dubbed "Calamity Corners" because of the number of accidents that occurred there. London annexed part of the township in 1961, bringing developers, new housing, retail strips, malls, and big-box stores. The Masonville branch of the London Public Library opened in 1995. Robert Mason's bones rest in London's Woodland Cemetery. He would not recognize the busy urban scene that bears his name.

Hilary Bates Neary

MCCLARY AVENUE

South. A dead-end avenue running west from Wellington Street.

At 53 McClary Avenue sits Beacon Lodge, built in 1864 for John McClary (1829-1921), owner of a stove works that was the largest employer in London from the 1890s to the 1940s. Across the street at 95 and 97 High Street are two identical cottages built in the 1870s for his daughters Theresa and Catherine and their husbands.

John McClary.

Originally founded by his brother Oliver, the business grew from a small tinware shop to a huge stove, furnace, and kitchen utensil maker with factories and warehouses across the country. Two factories oper-

The McClary cottages at 95 and 97 High Street, from the corner of McClary Avenue and High Street, circa 1890.

ated in London; one on the site of today's Galleria Mall and the other on Adelaide Street near the south branch of the Thames. A shrewd investor, McClary was president of London Life for over twenty-five years (1894-1920), and of Ontario Loan and Debenture (1894-1921).

Today, only the three family homes, all of which have been designated as architecturally and historically significant under the Ontario Heritage Act, recall McClary and his role in the development of London.

Mike Baker

MCCORMICK BOULEVARD

East. Runs north/south between Dundas Street and the Canadian Pacific Railway.

For almost ninety years, the large white factory at the corner of McCormick Boulevard and Dundas Street East has been churning out cookies, crackers, and candy. Built in 1914, and equipped with the latest in biscuit-making technology at the time, it was known as "the snow white sunshine biscuit and candy factory." The building has retained its large windows and original white-glazed terracotta exterior.

The factory was built by the McCormick Manufacturing Company, then under the direction of Thomas P. McCormick Jr., son of the founder. McCormick Sr. had left Ireland in 1849, landing in London in

The McCormick Manufacturing plant, Dundas Street East and McCormick Boulevard, 1914.

the early 1850s. Before his death in 1906, he founded the McCormick retirement home, which has remained at its original site, 230 Victoria Street. The McCormick brand can still be found on grocery shelves today.

Mike Baker

MCSTAY ROAD

Masonville. Runs east/west between Shavian Boulevard and Hillside Drive.

The McStays share a history with many families who left Ireland in the first decade of the nineteenth century for Madison County, New York, and later moved north to London Township. Betty McStay, a widow, arrived here in 1830 with her seven children. Her son James bought a two-hundred acre lot at the southwest corner of present-day Richmond Street and Fanshawe Park Road, where the family built a log house. James built a brick house facing Proof Line Road (later Richmond Street) about 1843, when most of his siblings had married and moved into homes of their own. It still stands, behind stately fir trees, at 1603 Richmond Street. The one-and-a-half storey white brick house is built on a centre-hall plan, with three gables that look out from the roof toward the busy traffic of Richmond Street. The land that James McStay once cultivated is now a subdivision of comfortable homes and winding streets, bordered on the north by Masonville School and a busy commercial corner.

Hilary Bates Neary

Meadowlily Bridge.

MEADOWLILY ROAD

Southeast. Runs north/south from Hamilton Road to Commissioners Road, east of Highbury Avenue.

Meadowlily Road brought farmers to the Meadow Lily Mills, the ruins of which can still be seen on the north side of the Thames River, east of the road. It is unknown when the first mill was constructed on the site, but a grist mill and sawmill called Shepherd's Mills occupied the 20-acre property by 1848. The operation was renamed Meadow Lily Mills in 1856. The mill's machinery was powered by river water. Twice the mills were rebuilt after serious fires, in 1885 and 1891. A mill continued to operate on this site until 1901, when it was again destroyed by fire and never restored.

A visitor today can see the old foundation stones and remains of the mill race. Look carefully and you will find the indentation of the mill pond and some structural remnants of the mill dam. The present-day Meadowlily Bridge was built in 1910. It was closed to traffic in 1962 and is now used only by pedestrians and cyclists.

Glen Curnoe

Waters' mill *by James Hamilton, circa 1850.*

MILL STREET

Central. Runs east/west between Richmond Street and Talbot Street.

Around 1832, Thomas Waters purchased land from John Stiles and built grist and sawmills on English's (later Carling) Creek where it joined the Thames River north of the village. The thick pine forest provided timber for his saw, and the grain of London's first settlers, grist for his mill. In 1843, James Hamilton, a Saturday artist with an eye for river scenes, painted a watercolour of Waters' mill operating with an overshot wheel and a flume bringing water from the creek.

    The mill was abandoned soon after and, by 1851, a syndicate, whose members included Elijah Leonard and John Carling, had Waters' property surveyed for streets and building lots. Waters turns up in local records concerning other mill developments, then disappears from history.

Glen Curnoe

MOUNT PLEASANT AVENUE

West. Runs east/west from Wilson Avenue to Riverside Drive.

In 1874, some prominent businessmen formed a voluntary association to establish a non-denominational public cemetery west of the city. Mount Pleasant Cemetery opened in a park-like setting in 1875. On Sunday afternoons, families and friends in mourning walked or rode in carriages to gather at Mount Pleasant, sometimes even picnicking while remembering loved ones. W.E. Saunders, a noted naturalist and devoted planter of trees, was responsible for much of the early landscaping. He introduced many Carolinian species, including cucumber, tulip, Osage orange, redbud, and a showy magnolia (near the Chapel). Today native trees such as the large copper beech near Riverside Drive display glorious autumn colour. Many trees bear identifying labels.

Before the cemetery opened, Mount Pleasant Avenue was known as Walker Street, named for Colonel John Walker, who created a subdivision in the 1870s between that street and the Thames River on the west side of Wharncliffe Road. He named the other streets after trees, of which only Walnut Street survives today. Mount Pleasant now ends at Riverside Drive, which was extended east to meet what was then Dundas Street West at Wharncliffe in the 1970s, following completion of the Queens Avenue bridge. Almost 30 homes were acquired and demolished to allow Riverside to pass through.

Netta Brandon

NORTH ROUTLEDGE PARK

North. Runs west from Hyde Park Road.

Hyde Park's first side street was opened in 1967 and named Routledge Street after Thomas and Elizabeth Routledge, the village's founders, who settled there in the summer of 1818 from Bewcastle, Cumberland County, England. They were among the first settlers in London Township, which had just been opened to settlement that year. The family owned several hundred acres of land on the northwest corner of the hamlet, perhaps named after the park in London, England. Descendants of the family were residents of Hyde Park until 1967. Margaret, the eldest of the pioneer couple's three daughters and six

Looking east along Gainsborough Road toward Hyde Park Road, circa 1915.

sons, was married in 1820 to Thomas Carling, who founded the Carling brewery in London in 1843. Theirs was the first marriage in London Township.

Routledge Street was renamed North Routledge Park in 1996 to avoid confusion with a street in Lambeth after both streets became part of London in the 1993 annexation.

George DeKay

O'BRIEN STREET

South. Runs southeast/northwest from Riverview Avenue to the Thames River.

Born in 1792 at Fermoy, Cork County, Ireland, Dennis O'Brien came to Upper Canada by way of the United States in 1820. In 1826, with the establishment of London as the administrative centre of the London District, O'Brien became the town's first general merchant, locating his store and residence on the south side of Dundas Street, between Ridout and Talbot Streets. Typical of pioneer merchants, O'Brien soon branched out into related enterprises. In 1835, he purchased a grist mill called Blackfriars at the foot of Kent Street in what is now Harris Park. Later, he operated a distillery across the river in Westminster Township. O'Brien also engaged in land speculation.

In the early 1850s, O'Brien accumulated property on the Westminster side of the Thames River, west of Wharncliffe Road, where he built "Riverview," a two-storey, brick residence. O'Brien died there in 1865. His daughter Mary, widow of Duncan McMillen, continued to live at Riverview until she sold the property to the Salvation Army in the late 1890s. The house became the Salvation Army Rescue Home and evolved into the Bethesda Salvation Army Hospital. It was replaced, a few years ago, by a modern structure that features, over the front door, a stained glass transom salvaged from the O'Brien house.

Dan Brock

PAARDEBERG CRESCENT

East. Runs east from Rhine Avenue.

The Battle of Paardeberg, February 18-27, 1900, marked a turning point for British fortunes in the South African (Boer) War. The attack was part of a strategy developed by a new British commander-in-chief, Frederick Sleigh, Lord Roberts, to relieve two besieged garrisons at Ladysmith and Mafeking by attacking the Boer capitals of Pretoria and Bloemfontein. Paardeberg marked the first time that Canadian soldiers fought overseas as a distinctly Canadian unit and it inspired future Canadian participation in the wars of the twentieth century — the two world wars, the Korean War, and many United Nations operations. The Paardeberg unit, the 2nd (Special Service) Battalion, Royal Canadian Regiment (RCR), received a battle honour for its service. News of this Canadian victory was received with a standing ovation in the Canadian House of Commons.

Paardeberg demonstrated that luck is an important element in battlefield success and that wars are always costly. More than 120 members of the RCR were injured and thirty were killed. The battle has become a regimental icon, symbolizing the grit and determination of Canadian infantrymen. For most of the twentieth century, London was the home station for the Royal Canadian Regiment.

A.M.J. Hyatt

Troops leaving for the Boer War marching south on Richmond Street toward Dundas Street, 1899.

The Crystal Palace exhibition hall near Central Avenue, circa 1875.

PALACE STREET

Central. Runs north/south from Princess Avenue to Central Avenue.

The area around Palace Street was surveyed and subdivided into building lots in 1851 by Samuel Peters Junior. Palace Street is named after the Crystal Palace, which was located in Hyde Park, London, England. Designed by Sir Joseph Paxton, the imposing iron structure was enclosed in one million feet of glass and was the showpiece of the Great Exhibition of 1851. "Crystal Palace" soon became a popular name for exhibit halls everywhere.

Two exhibition buildings in nineteenth-century London were named the "Crystal Palace," although they were constructed more of brick and wood than glass. The first was an octagonal structure built in 1861 on the fairgrounds, which were then located just north of today's Victoria Park. When the Western Fair moved to its present-day site in 1887, the building was disassembled and the materials sold. A new Crystal Palace was built at Queens Park and opened for the fair in September of that year. It was destroyed by fire in 1927.

Glen Curnoe

22 Peter Street.

PETER(S) STREET

Central. Runs north/south from Queens Avenue to Dufferin Avenue.

Samuel Peters Sr. (c. 1790-1864), who once owned land in the area of Peter Street, was born in Merton, Devonshire, England. He immigrated to London, Upper Canada (Ontario), with his wife and children in 1835 and, by 1840, was operating an abattoir near Ridout and Horton Streets. In 1850, he purchased a distillery near Blackfriars Bridge, situated on a large block of land which he soon subdivided and sold as building lots. The area later became part of Petersville, a short-lived municipality that was soon renamed London West. It amalgamated with the city in 1898.

In 1853, Peters built a country mansion known as Grosvenor Lodge at 1017 Western Road. The imposing Tudor Revival mansion was designed by his nephew, an architect also named Samuel Peters. It is now the London Regional Resource Centre for Heritage and the Environment.

The "s" was dropped from the street name as early as 1863 for the sake of convenience. A cement sidewalk stamped with the street name and the date 1902 can still be seen on the east side.

Glen Curnoe

POND MILLS ROAD

Southeast. Runs north/south between Southdale Road and Commissioners Road.

In the early nineteenth century, a small rural community developed in Westminster Township around a mill built near two kettle lakes that had been formed by retreating glaciers some 13,000 years ago. Thomas Waters, a United Empire Loyalist from New Brunswick, built the gristmill in the ravine just west of the north pond about 1823-24. The mill was constructed of oak timbers on a foundation of fieldstone and powered with water brought from the upper pond. Waters soon moved to the nearby settlement of London and built more mills near the Thames River. Thomas Baty, a settler from Northumberland, England, took over the Westminster mill. He and one of his sons, Robert, played an important role in the agricultural community that surrounded the ponds. Their family and neighbours are buried in the cemetery overlooking the north pond.

The mill continued to grind grain until 1934, but is now in ruins. The iron penstock that brought water to power the overshot wheel and run the heavy grindstones now protrudes from the side of the ravine. Ducks and muskrats live in a small pond below, where nature is reclaiming a piece of London's industrial heritage. But the beauty of these ponds is unchanged and still invites us to walk around their peaceful shores.

Hilary Bates Neary

Pond Mills.

PROUDFOOT LANE

West. Runs northwest/southeast from Beaverbrook Avenue across Oxford Street to the continuation of Beaverbrook Avenue.

Reverend William Proudfoot.

The Reverend William Proudfoot (1788-1851) was a Scottish preacher and teacher who immigrated to Upper Canada in 1832 with his wife, Isobel Aitchison (1789-1866) and six of their children. Proudfoot served as a Secessionist Church of Scotland missionary in London Township, Westminster Township, and Goderich. In London, his United Presbyterian congregation evolved into today's First St. Andrew's United Church and (New) St. James Presbyterian Church. He opened London's first divinity school in 1844 and trained his son John in the Presbyterian ministry.

Following the Rebellion of 1837, James Aitchison, Mrs. Proudfoot's nephew, was taken prisoner during a Patriot raid on Windsor in December 1838. William Proudfoot petitioned Sir George Arthur, the lieutenant-governor, for clemency for Aitchison. Many rebels were hanged in London after summary trials, but Aitchison was among those banished to Van Dieman's Land.

To support his large family, Proudfoot also farmed a two-hundred-acre lot, the eastern boundary of which is today's Proudfoot Lane. There his family's large log house was raised by friends in a riotous two-day bee that Proudfoot described in his diary, commending the hard workers and condemning the hard drinkers. Proudfoot's trenchant judgments on his life and times were published by the London and Middlesex Historical Society as *The Proudfoot Papers, 1832-1848.*

Netta Brandon

RANSON DRIVE AND SLEIGHTHOLME AVENUE

Northwest. Ranson Drive links Middlewoods Crescent and Heathcote Avenue. Sleightholme runs north/south from Sarnia Road to Rolling-wood Circle.

The Orchard Park subdivision recalls the Sleight family's acres of apple trees. Ranson Drive passes the 1940s house built by Harold Ranson Sleight, whose grandfather, Joseph Sleight, immigrated to Canada West in 1857, obtaining a farm on the third Concession, where he planted Spy apple trees. Apples were an essential fruit for early settlers. Weather conditions and soils were ideal for the crop; and the fruit stored well, could be dried, pressed into cider, and added to preserves.

Joseph's son, Frederick Ranson Sleight (1867-1943) grew up here. He bought Lot 19 in the late 1920s, moving into the house that still stands at the corner of Sarnia Road and Sleightholme Avenue with his wife, Martha Coombs, and their three adult sons. Harold kept dairy cattle on both properties, supplying milk to West London. His brothers, Gilbert and Ted, developed an extensive orchard business, introducing dwarf apple trees to the district, the Mutsu variety becoming very popular. The dairy operation was relocated in 1956 when the family property was purchased for Orchard Park, but Harold and Vera stayed, enjoying retirement as the subdivision grew up around them.

Netta Brandon

An apple tree on Ranson Drive.

City hall on Richmond Street looking south toward King Street, circa 1910.

RICHMOND STREET

A major north/south road beginning at the bridge over the south branch of the Thames, passing through city centre, northern neighbourhoods, across the north branch of the Thames, and up through Middlesex and Huron Counties (until recently Highway 4).

Richmond Street takes its name from Charles Lennox, 4th Duke of Richmond, Governor-in-Chief of the Canadas from July 1818 until he died in August 1819 from the bite of a rabid fox. He was also the brother-in-law of Lord Bathurst, and father-in-law of Sir Peregrine Maitland, whose names were given to other London streets. In London's early years the street had little significance, but in 1849 a joint stock company was formed to "grade, macadamize and bridge the Proof Line Road." This company chose Richmond rather than Wharncliffe as its route from downtown London into the Township, and made substantial improvements to the whole route from Dundas Street north, much to the relief of travellers, local farmers, and municipal councils; and its shareholders profited from the tolls charged.

A retrospective journey up Richmond Street is a trip through London's history. Beginning at Labatt's Brewery, past a synagogue, factories, the Grand Opera House, the Masonic Temple, Tecumseh's Hotel (refreshing its baseball players), City Hall, Smallman and Ingram's department store, banks, cathedrals and churches, schools, a magnificent art-deco post office, the Western Hotel (where the Donnelly stage coach stopped), the Military reservation (later the Fairgrounds), a classic CPR station, homes both modest and grand, hospitals, and an orphanage, shops and taverns, toll-gates, the gates to The University of Western Ontario, a mill-race, Sir Casimir Gzowski's graceful bridge below the convent, to the commercial and residential edge of London's northward sprawl: Richmond Street has seen it all.

Hilary Bates Neary

Dundas Street, south side, looking east from Richmond Street during the 1890s.

ROBIN'S HILL ROAD

Northeast. Runs east/west from Huron Street to Middlesex Road 27.

Despite a name that conjures up an image of spring birds, Robin's Hill Road has a more prosaic origin. Its namesake is Robin's Hill Cemetery, a pioneer burial ground opened in 1830 by the Scatcherd family, founders of the hamlet of Wyton in neighbouring West Nissouri Township. The Scatcherd brothers, John and Thomas, had immigrated to the wilds of Nissouri from Yorkshire, England, in the early 1820s. They settled on land through which the Wye River flowed on its way to the north branch of the Thames. A small community developed around the Scatcherd farms and grist mill, and inns and small manufactories were established nearby. The rail line from London to Stratford went through Wyton in the 1880s. Many members of the Scatcherd family and their neighbours — Talbots, Duffins, Evans, Clarks — are buried in that peaceful cemetery. Somewhere in Yorkshire there is a Robin's Hill that inspired this place of rest.

Alice Gibb

Robin's Hill Cemetery.

A horse-drawn pumper flies down King Street past the firehall, circa 1890.

ROE STREET

South. Runs north/south off Dowell Road, west of White Oak Road.

Fire ignited the Sterling Boot and Shoe factory in the early morning of January 6, 1904. Firefighters from the central fire hall on King Street responded to the call. On arrival they found the four-storey brick building on the northeast corner of York and Clarence Streets engulfed in flames. To train water into the building, firemen erected a fifty-five-foot ladder against the south façade. Just then, nearly half of the wall buckled and fell, burying Chief John Roe and four firefighters in tons of brick. Firemen and spectators scrambled to pull them from the debris. Two men went to hospital, and two were soon well enough to return to fighting the fire. But an eight-foot section of wall had caught Roe full in the face, and he died at the scene. The following Friday, thousands of Londoners lined the streets in a snowstorm as Roe's casket made its way to Mount Pleasant Cemetery, passing the central fire hall where the firemen saluted their beloved commander.

The Sterling factory was rebuilt on the stone foundation that survived the fire and, today, is one of only two surviving Clarence Street factory buildings.

Mike Baker

SANATORIUM ROAD

West. Runs north/south from Oxford Street to the Byron Bridge.

At the turn of the century, tuberculosis, a disease of the respiratory system, was the leading cause of death in Ontario. Organizations were formed to build facilities, known as sanatoria, for the treatment of patients who needed rest and fresh air to make a recovery. In London, Adam Beck, former mayor, hospital trustee, and chairman of Ontario Hydro, took the lead. He formed, along with several other prominent Londoners, the London Health Association (LHA) and raised money to build and equip a sanatorium, which opened in 1910 on a former farm overlooking the Thames River near Byron. Over the next seventy years, thousands of patients were treated at the "San."

The fight against tuberculosis was won in the years following the Second World War with the introduction of antibiotics such as streptomycin, and the San's extensive facilities were no longer needed. Much of the surrounding land was sold to the London Hunt and Country Club, and the facility itself was sold to the province in 1959. The LHA leased back some space in order to continue serving their remaining patients. The rest of the site was then taken over by the Children's Psychiatric Research Institute (now the Child and Parent Resource Institute).

Sir Adam Beck.

Detail of the Pratten Building at the former Beck Sanatorium.

St. Luke's-in-the-Garden Chapel on the grounds of the Child and Parent Resource Institute, the former Beck Sanatorium.

While continuing to operate reduced facilities at the old San, the LHA decided in the early 1960s to build a teaching hospital at The University of Western Ontario in conjunction with the planned move of the medical school from Victoria Hospital to the campus. In 1972, the LHA's new University Hospital was opened by famous Canadian neurosurgeon Dr. Wilder Penfield.

Mike Baker

Sandy Somerville at the London Hunt and Country Club on Richmond Street in the mid-1930s.

SANDY SOMERVILLE DRIVE AND PLACE

West. RiverBend. Sandy Somerville Drive is located north of Kains Road and skirts the RiverBend Golf Course.

RiverBend, located west of Byron, includes a private eighteen-hole golf course combined with various types of living accommodations across the river from the London Hunt and Country Club. Inside its gates, RiverBend's streets honour prominent local amateur golfers such as Jack Nash, Ed Ervasti, and Sandy Somerville.

C. Ross (Sandy) Somerville was an all-round athlete who excelled in badminton, cricket, football, and hockey, but his most outstanding accomplishments were in golf. After winning the Canadian amateur championship six times and, in 1932, the United States amateur championship, he was selected as Golfer of the Half-Century (1900-50) and inducted into the Canadian Sports Hall of Fame, the Royal Canadian Golf Association Hall of Fame, and the Ontario Golf Association Hall of Fame.

Dr. Howie Cameron

SIMCOE STREET

Col. John Graves Simcoe.

Central. Runs east/west from Hamilton Road to Talbot Street.

John Graves Simcoe (1752-1806) was the founder of London and arguably the city's most significant historical figure. Simcoe's energetic service as a regimental commander during the American Revolution cemented his reputation for military skill and personal valour. His great wealth (acquired through marriage) and political connections fuelled his personal ambition to restore British supremacy in North America. His service was finally rewarded in 1791 when he was made the first lieutenant-governor of Upper Canada.

Simcoe argued that, if the capital of Upper Canada were built in what is now Western Ontario, the British could extend their strategic alliance with Native tribes in American territory. On March 2-3, 1793, Simcoe made a brief, but now celebrated, visit to the Forks of the Thames River. He decided that this was to be the site of "new" London and made immediate plans for a permanent settlement.

Unfortunately for London, military pressure from the United States and lack of support from Simcoe's superiors forced the establishment of a capital at York, now Toronto. The settlement of London was thus postponed until 1826.

Simcoe Street dates from the original 1826 survey of London. On it can be found one of London's most poignant but least-known cenotaphs. West of Wellington Street, on a city boulevard in front of an apartment building, rests the only remaining evidence of the long-ago demolished Simcoe Street elementary school: a small stone marker that commemorates the sons of neighbourhood families who were killed during the First World War.

John Mombourquette

Victoria Hospital, South Street, pictured in the early 1900s.

SOUTH STREET

Central. Runs east/west from the south branch of the Thames River to Adelaide Street.

In 1905, City Council received a petition to change South Street's name to Ottaway Avenue, in honour of Lillian Ottaway, wife of Adam Beck and a dedicated volunteer for Victoria Hospital, which was located on South Street. Council gave its approval, but County Judge Talbot Macbeth turned down the City's application on the grounds that he could see no "reason for changing the name of South to Ottaway as proposed." What was not mentioned at the time, but whispered decades later by certain locals, was "that there was more to this than appeared on the surface — Macbeth it was said was not an admirer of Beck."

Nonetheless, Ottaway Avenue became the popular name for South Street, and the city directories, beginning in 1908, referred to the street as such. The London Street Railway even ran an Ottaway Avenue street car. This situation lasted until late 1947, when city clerk Reg Cooper insisted that South Street was not Ottaway Avenue. Sometime later, city engineer Roy Garrett started posting South Street signs on what was generally known as Ottaway Avenue, and the change was accepted by local residents.

Dan Brock

The miniature train in Springbank Park.

SOUTH WENIGE DRIVE

North. Runs south from Sunningdale Road.

George Wenige (1874-1952) the former London mayor who holds the record for most election victories, has had a hard time holding onto a street. His first election win was in 1923, shortly after he finished building his new bicycle store on Wellington Street, north of Dundas Street. His last win was in 1950, and there were seven others in between.

 The city first attempted to rename Byron Avenue in Wenige's honour, but the residents opposed it. During the 1970s and 1980s, Highway 126 was known as the Wenige Expressway, but it is now simply called Highbury Avenue South. The north end of London has proved a more secure location for Wenige to date. The first part of South Wenige Drive was registered in 2001; there will be a North Wenige Drive when development starts north of Sunningdale Road.

Mike Baker

SPRINGBANK DRIVE

West. Runs east/west from Wharncliffe Road, to the intersection of Base Line Road and Commissioners Road.

About 1845, Charles Coombs purchased McEwen's grist mill, known as the Spring Mill, roughly where Storybook Gardens is today. It was powered by spring water collected in three ponds. Coombs, and later his sons, Henry and John, ran the mill until 1878, when the City of London acquired the property. A dam was built across the river and a pumping station on the mill site, which pumped spring water into a reservoir on top of Chestnut or Hungerford (now Reservoir) Hill. A pipeline was laid from the reservoir to the city to supply London's growing demand for fresh, clean water. This right of way was made into a road that was called Pipe Line Road.

During the next few decades, the city bought additional land along the river, both to add more springs to its water supply and to expand the parkland available to its citizens. Steamboats brought Londoners from the Forks to the park for a day of sylvan walks and picnics. In 1896, the London Street Railway extended its rails to Springbank Park. With the advent of the automobile, driving through the park became a popular pastime and, in 1948, Pipe Line Road was renamed Springbank Drive.

Hilary Bates Neary

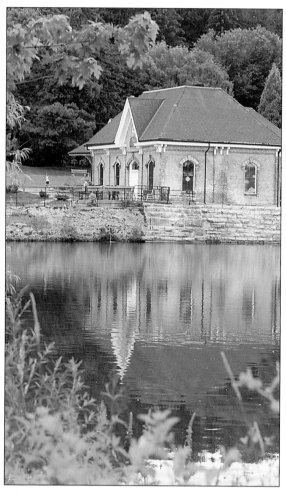

The pumphouse in Springbank Park.

ST. JULIEN STREET

Southeast. Runs north/south from the south branch of the Thames River to Trafalgar Street.

In the twenty-first century, few would remember the connection between a Canadian park and street and a small Belgian village northeast of Ypres. The village of St. Julien, populated by seven hundred citizens in 1915, became the focus of attention for the First Canadian Division in the spring of that year. The Battle for St. Julien (April 24-25, 1915) was part of the "Second Battle of Ypres" of the First World War, and notorious for the introduction of poison gas as a weapon.

Twice during this battle the German forces released a cloud of chlorine gas, and both times the Canadians played an important role in halting the German advance. The official British communiqué for the battle noted that, "Canadians had many casualties but their gallantry and determination undoubtedly saved the situation." St. Julien could not be held after the second attack, however, and by the end of the fighting, the village was well behind the German front line.

For their efforts at St. Julien Canadians won four Victoria Crosses and suffered more than six thousand casualties.

A.M.J. Hyatt

STANLEY STREET

Central. Runs east/west from Westminster Bridge to Wharncliffe Road.

Stanley Street was named for Edward Stanley (1799-1869), Colonial Secretary in 1833-34 and 1841-45. He was a man of great influence, deciding where regiments were stationed and who received colonial governorships. He served as prime minister three times: in 1852, 1858-59, and 1866-68.

As the fourteenth Earl of Derby, Stanley was born into the English aristocracy, starting his political life on the left and moving to the right over his lifetime. In 1830, he joined the Whig administration under Lord Grey and supported the Reform Act of 1832. In 1833, as Colonial Secretary, he led the fight to abolish slavery. In 1834, Stanley broke with the Whigs over the reform of the Irish Church, and joined the Tories under Sir Robert Peel in 1841, returning to the Colonial Office. In 1845, he broke with Peel over the Corn Laws and emerged as the leader of the Tory Party's protectionist rump. Prime minister when the British North America Act was legislated, Stanley was truly a Father of Confederation. The fame of his family name in Canada, however, owes more to his second son, the sixteenth Earl of Derby, who was the Stanley behind the Stanley Cup.

Fred Dreyer

Cottages built by Anthony Steels on Patricia Street.

STEELE STREET

Broughdale. Runs west from Waterloo Street across Patricia Street and ends in a cul-de-sac.

The Steels house at 1057 Waterloo Street.

In 1905, Anthony Steels, master builder, bought eight acres on the west side of Waterloo Street in the community of Broughdale, (*see* **BROUGHDALE AVE**) where he built himself a large and handsome house (1057 Waterloo Street today). He established a workshop in the garden and built a barn where he kept several cows and some chickens for his own use.

In 1914, he registered a plan to subdivide his property. The surveyor, Frederick W. Farncomb, named the two streets on the subdivision plan. One was Steels Street — known as Steele Street today. The other was Patricia Street, named after Her Royal Highness, Princess Patricia of Connaught, the daughter of Canada's Governor-General and namesake of the Princess Patricia's Canadian Light Infantry, raised in 1914. Anthony Steels built many of the homes in his small subdivision himself. Some residents of Broughdale criticized him for building cottages instead of "proper" houses, but Steels felt there was a need for affordable homes on the market "to give young folks starting out a chance." These cottages can still be seen on Steele and Patricia Streets today (1042, 1044, 1046 Patricia Street).

Jo Shawyer

STEVENSON AVENUE

East. Runs north from Trafalgar Street and east from Hale Street.

Dr. Hugh Allan Stevenson, a well-known London physician, made a name for himself in the community through his profession, his philanthropic endeavours, and his political life. He served on a number of civic boards and as London mayor three times. In the mayor's race of 1916, he tied his opponent in the vote count and was elected by the vote of the city clerk, beating industrialist William M. Gartshore. But it was in 1919 that his name came to prominence, not only in London but throughout the Province of Ontario. When the founder of Ontario Hydro, Sir Adam Beck, MPP for London, broke with the Conservative Party and ran as an independent, Dr. Stevenson ran against him for the Independent Labour Party, a social-democratic political organization born in London in 1896. To the shock of political observers everywhere, the "Hydro Knight" was defeated by Dr. Stevenson.

David Spencer

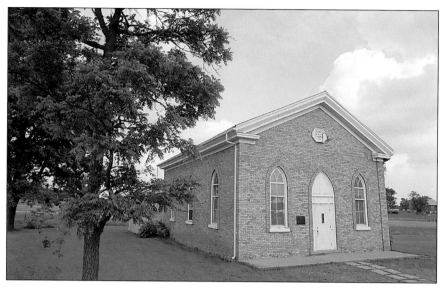

Tempo Presbyterian Church.

TEMPO ROAD

South. Runs north/south from Littlewood Drive to Colonel Talbot Road.

The hamlet of Tempo once flourished at the corner of Tempo and Colonel Talbot Roads. Mr. Abraham Ramey opened the first post office in June 1864, but the hamlet was named by a resident, Thomas Weldon, who came from Tempo, County Fermanagh, Ireland. The word is said to mean "right-hand turn" in Irish and may refer to a clockwise turn toward the sun in an ancient pagan ritual.

In 1895, Tempo's business community included two florists, a blacksmith, apiarist, carpenter, livestock seller, butcher, painter, dressmaker, general store/post office proprietor, and a barber who sold cigars on the side. In 1913, the post office closed and, by 1947, only the store, school, and church were left.

Most of what remained of Tempo was torn down when Highway 401 was built. In the spring of 1956, Tempo School was demolished to allow for the cloverleaf ramp formation at Highway 4, an unfortunate loss since it was one of the oldest one-room schools in the township. Tempo Presbyterian Church, still used for services, is among the few remaining traces of the forgotten village.

Jennifer Grainger

Identifying bodies at the Sulphur Springs following the sinking of the steamboat Victoria *in 1881.*

THAMES STREET

Central. Runs north/south from Horton Street to King Street.

One of London's earliest streets, Thames Street, was named for its proximity to the Thames River. And, thanks to its propensity to flood in earlier times, the river was occasionally part of the street. Consequently, most houses on the street were quite modest, including

Thames Street looking south from King Street during the 1937 flood.

many wooden double houses, none of which survived. Over the years, the inhabitants shared their street with the jail yard, the police station, a laundry, a foundry, Penmans woollen underwear factory, and two steam-driven electrical power plants.

Near the Forks of the Thames, the street once bordered the grounds of the Sulphur Springs, a health spa that attracted visitors from as far away as the United States. From a wharf next to the spa, steamers departed regularly for Springbank Park. When one of them, the *Victoria*, broke up and sank on May 24, 1881, the dead were brought to the Forks on another steamer and laid out on the Sulphur Springs grounds to be identified by grieving family members.

Mike Baker

TOOHEY LANE

North. Runs south off Ambleside Drive.

On the evening of June 24, 1898, an escaped convict from Georgetown, Texas jumped off an eastbound freight onto the tracks near Waterloo Street. He assaulted a night watchman who challenged him and fled toward Ontario Street, where police constable Michael Toohey tried to arrest him. The culprit, later identified as Marion Brown, pulled a gun and shot the constable twice. Toohey died almost instantly from a stomach wound.

Brown might have gotten away with murder, but he left two clues behind: his hat, later identified by a Texas jailer, and the print of his wooden left leg in the earth. He was apprehended almost six months later in Washington state, and returned to London where his seven-day trial produced a death sentence.

On May 17, 1899, well hidden from the public, Brown was hanged from a borrowed scaffold on the grounds of the old jail.

Peg Leg Brown.

Buried in the jail yard, some of his remains were accidentally unearthed 80 years later by a backhoe working on the new court-house parking lot. "Peg Leg" Brown was identified by his missing lower left leg. Today his wooden leg is on exhibit in the Forks of the Thames Museum Centre at 1 Dundas Street.

Mike Baker

Tozer's Shell Station at Mount Pleasant Avenue and Wharncliffe Road during the 1937 flood.

TOZER AVENUE

West. Runs east/west between Woodward Avenue and Upper Avenue.

Leonard Tozer (1893-1945) was the owner of the Shell service station at the corner of Mount Pleasant Avenue and Wharncliffe Road North in 1937 when it was swamped by the Thames River flood. Around 1940, he joined his neighbours at a meeting to discuss naming local streets. Charles Foster suggested that the road beside the considerable Tozer property, now 26 Woodward Avenue, carry the family's name. Good neighbours to each other, Leonard countered that the Foster name should also grace a street, and both names were used.

Mrs. Leonard Tozer, now one hundred years of age, converted the family home to three apartments and remained there until recent years. The house is still in full use. Her daughter and son-in-law built on part of the property, and raised their family as the fourth generation on Tozer land.

Netta Brandon

WATSON STREET

South. A dead end street running east from Wellington Road.

George Watson, a carpenter from England, immigrated to Canada in 1833 with his wife, Margaret. In 1843, he held the position of town carpenter and maintained London's wooden sidewalks. He bought land in 1855 at the southeast corner of what is now Watson Street and Wellington Road South, where he built a house.

In 1905, when Watson was 93, a *London Free Press* reporter recorded his reminiscences about London in 1833. "The whole of what was called London in those days lay along Ridout Street and consisted for the most part a few small shanties," Watson said. A former volunteer firefighter, he recalled being "armed with leather buckets… The fire engine was a primitive affair, with a long bar on each side which was manned by as many as could grasp it and worked violently up and down." The fire engine was destroyed in the Great Fire of 1845, which Watson vividly remembered fighting.

Glen Curnoe

WAVELL STREET

East. Runs east/west between Hale Street and Dundas Street.

Archibald Wavell was born into a military family and, by age eighteen, was commissioned an officer in the British Army. He served in the Boer War and the First World War, losing his left eye at the Battle of Ypres and earning a promotion to a command position with the British army in Palestine. When the Second World War began in 1939, Wavell's job as General Officer Commanding, and later Commander-in-Chief, was to protect the Suez Canal and prevent the region's oil riches from falling into Axis hands. Over a quarter of a million Italian soldiers attacked Egypt from Libya on September 13, 1940, halting on September 16 after a seventy-mile advance to the main British offensive line. On December 9, Wavell launched a "five-day raid" in which his 63,000 troops advanced 500 miles and captured 130,000 prisoners, prompting the Foreign Secretary, Anthony Eden, to quip: "Never has so much been surrendered by so many to so few."

Wavell never again had the same success in battle. An Italo-German attack in April, 1941 drove the British back to Egypt, and eventually cost Wavell his command. He was transferred to various positions in India and southeast Asia, but was fobbed off with a political appointment as Viceroy of India in 1943 after failing to stop the Japanese invasion of Burma. He died in England in 1950.

Jonathan Vance

Webster House on Kilally Road.

WEBSTER STREET

Northeast. Runs north/south from Huron Street, east of Highbury Avenue, to Kilally Road.

The Webster family were English Wesleyan Methodists descended from a soldier in Cromwell's army who settled in County Wicklow, Ireland. They were deeply loyal to the Crown and their Protestant faith. In 1811, when sectarian troubles repeatedly threatened his family, Robert Webster, his wife Elizabeth, and their two sons joined the exodus of Anglo-Irish families heading for Eaton, Madison County, New York. After the War of 1812, some of these families, including the Websters, moved on to Upper Canada.

Following his arrival in 1819, Webster was located by Thomas Talbot on the north half of Lot 7, Concession 3, London Township. The Webster stone homestead still stands on the corner of present-day Sandford Street and Kilally Road. In 1826, a neighbour, Joseph Percival, donated land for a graveyard and a Methodist mission church

•

and school on Huron Street facing Webster's land. Formerly the
Webster Cemetery, it is now called the Grove Cemetery. Many
Websters and the families whose journeys they shared from Ireland to
London — Beltons, Dickensons, Kernohans, Needhams, Tackaberrys,
and Wheatons — rest in that peaceful place.

Hilary Bates Neary

WELLINGTON GARDENS

Enters the development from Wellington Street between Regent Street
and Victoria Street.

Each May during the 1950s, *The London Free Press* would announce the
opening of what was once the most popular private garden in London.
Thousands would take the opportunity to drive through the grounds of
Morgan Gardens, marvelling at the hundreds of species of tulips and
the many cutting beds filled with perennials, including lemon day lilies,
narcissus, grape hyacinth, blue bells, golden alyssum, phlox, and crown
imperials.

The Gardens were the property of Andrew Morgan, a successful seed
merchant, incubator manufacturer, and poultry-supply dealer. In 1921,
he built a new house on Wellington Street just south of Regent Street
and continued to ornament his extensive grounds, which covered the
northern two-fifths of the block. By the late 1920s, visitors could enter
the gardens in their cars, tour the grounds, and exit onto Waterloo
Street. The gardens declined in popularity in the years just before
Morgan's death in 1960.

Later that year, Richard and Beryl Ivey bought the house and
grounds. They replaced the old house with a more contemporary structure, and then turned to the gardens. Many elements of the original
gardens were saved, some in their original location, as the Ivey's own
distinctive grounds took shape.

In the early 1990s, the Iveys decided to sell their home at 990
Wellington Street. They acquired additional property to the south and
created a small subdivision called Wellington Gardens. Several
Regency-inspired one-storey houses have been completed, including
their own home at 960 Wellington Street. Today, one can still catch a
glimpse of a portion of the Morgan Gardens, adapted and restored by
the Iveys, behind their former home.

Mike Baker

Wellington Street looking north from Dufferin Avenue, circa 1910 (now the site of City Hall and Centennial Hall).

WELLINGTON STREET AND WELLINGTON ROAD

Central. Runs north/south from Huron Street to St. Thomas.

Arthur Wellesley, 1st Duke of Wellington (1769-1852) was arguably the greatest nineteenth-century British hero, the only other contender being Admiral Horatio Nelson, who died at the battle of Trafalgar on October 21, 1805. Nelson was hailed for saving Britain from Napoleon by sea, while Wellington was regarded as the military saviour of the country, the Empire, and monarchical and aristocratic Europe. Both were buried with huge monuments in St. Paul's Cathedral.

Wellington won impressive victories in India (where his oldest brother, Richard Colley, Marquis Wellesley and Earl of Mornington, was Governor-General) between 1797 and 1805, and in the Peninsular War (1808-14) to liberate Portugal and Spain from France, where he was successful against great odds and with limited resources. His fame spread following the Battle of Waterloo on June 18, 1815 when, for the first time, he fought Napoleon directly and emerged as "great by land as thou by sea," as Tennyson apostrophised the spirit of Nelson. For the remainder of his life, Wellington was regarded almost as an equal by the rulers of Europe.

From 1818-27, he was a member of the British Cabinet as Master General of the Ordnance, commanding the engineers and artificers as well as the artillery. Military officers appointed to colonial governments owed their offices as much to him as to his close colleague Lord Bathurst, Secretary of State for War and the Colonies, who never failed to consult the Duke. From 1828-30, Wellington served as prime minister and, in 1827 and from 1842 to his death, he was commander-in-chief of the British army. In Canada, Wellington is commemorated as a military hero and an important figure in the defence of the colonies after 1818.

Neville Thompson

Westminster Hospital in the early 1930s. Commissioners Road is to the right.

WESTMINSTER AVENUE

South. Runs north/south between Base Line Road and Thompson Road.

Two threads of London's history, the pioneer and the military, come together in Westminster Avenue. Shortly before the War of 1812, United Empire Loyalists, Americans, and families from the eastern parts of the Canadas began to settle on the rich lands to the south of the

Thames River in what became Westminster Township. When the first township council meeting was held in 1817 the thriving community claimed 428 citizens. Its gifts were so manifest that it was only a matter of time before the township was consumed by the city of London. What is now the old south was annexed in 1890, the area Westminster Avenue occupies in 1961, and the remainder in 1993.

The township disappeared in that final annexation, but by then it already had a namesake. During the First World War, the federal government scrambled to care for wounded soldiers and chose London for the site of a neuropsychiatric hospital, which was to accommodate (as a contemporary report put it) "soldiers whose nerves had been shattered." The new facility, erected on eighty acres of land between Wellington Road and the London & Port Stanley Railway, was called Westminster Hospital in honour of the township and accepted its first patients in April 1920. It became a general hospital in 1929, expanding considerably during the Second World War in order to treat another generation of war casualties. The Victoria Hospital Corporation acquired the largely rebuilt facility in 1977 and changed its name, but Westminster Avenue preserves the heritage, both of the original Westminster Hospital and the township in which it was situated.

Jonathan Vance

Westminster Tower, London Health Sciences Centre.

WESTON STREET

South. Runs east/west from Wellington Road to Fairview Avenue.

Weston Street is one of London's most researched streets. This is due mainly to the keenly focused interest of the late London artist Greg Curnoe.

Greg Curnoe and his family moved into 38 Weston Street in 1968. In 1990, a minor legal question concerning the boundaries of his property piqued his interest and provided the incentive for him to start looking into his lot's history. Greg always had a keen interest in local history and he found in his research that in most cases the subject of local histories placed emphasis on prominent families and public figures. He also found that historical accounts of the early settlement of this area favoured the perspective of the European settlers with very little reference to the First Nations' effect on the community.

Weston Street had been named for William Weston, who first bought property in the area in 1842. The building at 38 Weston Street was originally built in 1891 for Knowles & Co. Lithographers, a firm known for fine art prints and lithographed souvenir postcards. Later, the front of the building was made into an apartment and the former lithography plant was converted into a woodworking shop. It was an ideal set-up for Greg, as it provided both living accommodation for his family and a studio for his work.

From 1991 until his death in 1992, Greg intensified his research into the area in which he lived. He combed the neighbourhood for clues to its past. He talked to neighbours and relatives of past neighbours, and spent hours in local archives and the Middlesex County Registry Office. As librarian of the London Room, I helped him search through countless microfilm reels, books, and manuscripts. He eventually broadened his research to incorporate First Nations peoples of southwestern Ontario between 1750 and 1850. He consulted with First Nations descendants, from whom he received encouragement. He made use of collections at both the Ontario and National Archives. He even arranged to have an archaeological dig conducted on the back of his property.

Greg put together enough material for two books, *Deeds/abstracts: the History of a London Lot* and *Deeds/Nations*, which were published posthumously after his tragic death in 1992. His home at 38 Weston Street was designated under the Ontario Heritage Act in July 1993.

Glen Curnoe

WHARNCLIFFE ROAD

West. Runs north/south from Lambeth, ending near the north branch of the Thames.

Colonel Thomas Talbot commissioned Mahlon Burwell to survey the Wharncliffe Highway in the summer of 1824, two years before the town plot of London was laid out. Strategically located, Wharncliffe was designed to link growing settlements in Westminster Township with future ones in London Township. It also connected Longwoods Road to the west with Commissioners Road, a major east-west route.

Talbot named this road for an old friend, James Archibald Stuart-Wortley, whom he had known since 1791 when they were both young army officers stationed in Quebec City. Created Baron Wharncliffe of Wortley in 1826, he remained Talbot's closest English friend until his death. Wortley Road also honours him.

Burwell's route for the highway through London Township was also his proof line, serving as both a road allowance and as a check on the accuracy of his survey. North of Oxford Street (Concession 2), the line went straight through the Thames River valley — not a sensible route for a road. When Wharncliffe was actually laid out, it followed the high banks of the river, again meeting Burwell's Proof Line Road where Western Road now meets Richmond Street. The old planned connection is evident today in the path followed by Highway 4 through the city of London: it takes Richmond Street to the north and Wharncliffe Road to the south.

Douglas Leighton

WHISKER STREET

North. Runs north from Chambers Avenue.

Street names in London's suburbs have traditionally been the purview of developers who are often seeking to convey a particular image for the street or to commemorate people and places. Sifton Properties Limited, one of London's oldest and largest developers, decided to take a different approach when they began work on the Upland Hills subdivision in north London in 1999.

Sifton involved neighbourhood children in naming the streets of the new development through a contest held at nearby elementary schools.

Many of the street names suggested by the students reflected their own interests, such as pets, cartoon characters, and family members. One of the names selected was proposed by Melissa Panette in honour of her rabbit, Whisker. Melissa felt that Whisker, acquired when she moved to London, was "a very nice pet" and was important enough for a street to be named after him. Sifton agreed, and one of the first streets to be developed in Upland Hills was named Whisker. Other names chosen from the submissions included Firefly, Skyline, and Elderberry.

The warm and whimsical nature of the name is appropriate for a residential street inhabited by families with young children. Although Whisker the rabbit may some day depart to that great grassy knoll in the sky, Whisker Street will always remind at least one family of a beloved pet who held a special place in their hearts.

Maureen Zunti Jones

WHITE OAK ROAD

South. Runs north/south from Southdale Road to the County Line.

This South London road was named after the former hamlet of White Oak, once located at the corner of White Oak Road and Concession 4

White Oak United Church and graveyard.

(now Dingham Drive) in Westminster Township. The first post office, named for the white oak trees common to the area, opened under post-master John Archer in 1879. A blacksmith and the White Oak Cheese Factory also operated in the community.

Much of the rest of the village was scattered along White Oak Road to the south of this intersection. White Oak School was first built in the 1850s; its modern descendant is still standing near Highway 402, although it closed in 1965. The former White Oak waterworks, built in 1959, is across the road. The frame Union Bible Christian Church was built in 1875, became Methodist in 1884, and was bricked over in 1914. It became White Oak United Church in 1925. Although the graveyard is well-maintained, the church is empty, boarded-up, and deteriorating.

Jennifer Grainger

WILSON AVENUE

Central. Runs north/south from Riverside Drive to Blackfriars Street.

Dr. John D. Wilson, 1900.

The municipality of London West was amalga-mated with the city in 1898 during the term of Mayor John D. Wilson, a popular and public-spir-ited physician. He had entered the mayor's race to ensure that the new Victoria Hospital project was debated and, if he were elected, properly carried out. Though he opposed expansion of the old hos-pital, that option was endorsed by the public which elected him — both by wide margins. A memorial to Queen Victoria's sixty years on the throne, the extensive addition opened in November of 1899.

Following the amalgamation, all streets in West London with names identical to those in the city were renamed, and Centre Street became Wilson. Many of the new names came from other members of council including Wyatt, Cooper, and Carrothers.

In 1921, Wilson's son, John Cameron Wilson, was elected mayor. Ironically, he succeeded E.S. Little, the son of J.W. Little, the man who John D. Wilson succeeded as mayor in 1898.

Mike Baker

WILTON GROVE

South. Runs east/west from Wellington Road to the city limits.

Now in an industrial suburb of South London, this road once passed only farms on its way through the rural neighbourhood of Wilton Grove. The centre of this hamlet was near the intersection of present-day Wilton Grove Road and Pond Mills Road, just east of the London & Port Stanley Railway crossing. By 1856, the line's Westminster railway station was located on the north side of Wilton Grove Road, west of the tracks. Here was the first home of the Wilton Grove Post Office when it opened November 1, 1873, under William Hogg, the postmaster. Mail arrived on the train and was delivered by horse and buggy to nearby communities such as Hubrey and Pond Mills. In 1879, Peter Murray took over as postmaster and moved the office into his home. William Murray ran the post office from 1918 to 1957, receiving the Buckingham Palace Coronation Medal in 1953 for his long-standing service. The Wilton Grove Presbyterian (now United) Church is all that remains of this rural community.

Jennifer Grainger

WINDERMERE ROAD

North. Runs east/west from the Thames River east of Adelaide Street to the Medway Valley west of Ryerse Road.

Windermere Road is named after the first of several estates built by wealthy Londoners along its sylvan length. Daniel S. Perrin, a manufacturer of biscuits, gave the Windermere property overlooking the Medway Valley to his daughter, Elsie, on her marriage to Dr. Hadley Williams in 1903. In 1916, Elsie built a Spanish Colonial house, which was probably designed by London architect John M. Moore. She might have influenced its design and she certainly planned the whimsical gatehouse at its entrance. Elsie died in 1934, leaving Windermere to the city along with a large endowment for its maintenance as a museum and park, once her devoted housekeeper, Miss Harriet Corbett, who received lifetime occupancy, had passed away. The City successfully contested the will in the Ontario Supreme Court, and was thus able to use some of the endowment to build the Elsie Perrin Williams Memorial Library and Art Museum at 305 Queens Avenue in 1939.

Daniel S. Perrin playing tennis on the grounds of Windermere, his summer residence, circa 1905.

Miss Corbett lived on at Windermere until her death in 1979. For almost twenty years, the Heritage London Foundation has ensured that the estate remains a public facility.

Theresa Regnier and Hilary Bates Neary

WOLSELEY AVENUE

Central. Runs north/south between McMahen Street and Piccadilly Street.

Garnet Joseph, First Viscount Wolseley and Honorary Colonel of the Royal Canadian Regiment from 1899 until his death in 1913, was born in Ireland in 1833. He entered the army as an ensign in the 12th Regiment of Foot in March 1852, and was wounded at Sebastopol. He served in India and China before coming to Canada in 1861 as Assistant Quartermaster General. Wolseley commanded an expedition to Red River in August and September 1870 during the first Riel Rebellion, for which he was knighted. Wolseley also commanded relief forces that attempted to reach General Gordon at Khartoum. On this mission, he employed four hundred Canadian voyageurs, and Red River-type boats. Returning to England, he worked to modernize the army. In Gilbert & Sullivan's *The Pirates of Penzance*, Wolseley is mimicked as "the very model of a modern major general." He is buried in St. Paul's Cathedral and is honoured with an equestrian statue in the Horse Guards' Parade, Whitehall.

After the 1885 Riel Rebellion, a military school was established on Carling Heights, and the barracks were named after Garnet Wolseley. The barracks housed the Infantry School Corps, Canada's first regular force, which evolved into the Royal Canadian Regiment. A museum dedicated to the regiment now occupies part of the building.

Alastair Neely

Wolseley Barracks.

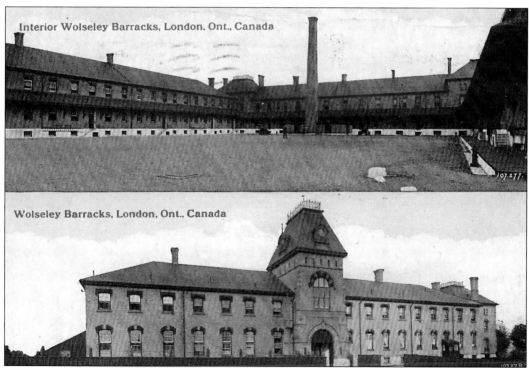

Wolseley Barracks in the early 1900s.

The dance floor at Wonderland in the early 1940s.

WONDERLAND ROAD

West. Runs north/south from Highway 7 to Elgin County Road 22.

In May 1935, the Wonderland Summer Gardens opened and quickly became a popular place for indoor and outdoor dancing, swimming, and fine dining. Run by brothers Charles and Wilford Jones, some of the biggest acts in music appeared on its stage. By 1956, the gravel driveway leading into the Gardens from Springbank Drive had evolved into Wonderland Side Road, which led south into Westminster Township.

Following annexation of the area in 1961, this rural road was gradually enveloped by urban sprawl. The nature of Wonderland changed forever with the opening of the Guy Lombardo Bridge in November 1978. Dismissed by contemporary critics as "the bridge to nowhere," this four-lane span over the Thames River linked Wonderland to the former Hutton Side Road, causing the Hutton name to almost disappear and creating one of the busiest north-south arteries in London.

Ironically, the decision to name the bridge after London's most famous musical son was based on the myth that Lombardo and his band, The Royal Canadians, played many of their first engagements at Wonderland Gardens. In truth, Lombardo only performed at the Gardens twice — more than thirty years after he became famous.

Christopher Doty

BIBLIOGRAPHY

The amateur and professional historian wishing to learn about the history of London is invited to haunt the collections of the London Room at the London Public Library and those of the J.J. Talman Regional Collection in The D.B. Weldon Library at The University of Western Ontario. Both maintain excellent resources for the study of local history: census records, assessment rolls, city directories, maps, newspaper clippings (LPL), Registered Plan Books (UWO), as well as books, pamphlets, and periodicals relating to the region.

Architectural Conservancy of Ontario Inc., London Region Branch. *Brackets and Bargeboards, London: Architectural Walks in London, Ontario*. London: Architectural Conservancy of Ontario, 1989.

Armstrong, Frederick H. *The Forest City: An Illustrated History of London, Canada*. Burlington: Windsor Publications, 1986.

Armstrong, Frederick H. and Daniel J. Brock. *Reflections on London's Past*. London: The Corporation of the City of London, 1975.

Baker, Michael, ed. *Downtown London: Layers of Time*. London: The City of London and London Regional Art and Historical Museums, 1998.

Bremner, Archibald. *City of London, Ontario, Canada: the Pioneer Period and the London of Today*. London: London Printing and Lithographing Company, 1900.

Brock, Daniel J. "Cyrenius Hall and the Byron Grist and Flour Mills," London Public Library and Art Museum Occasional Paper No. 24, *A Miscellany of London*, part 2, 1978.

Buchanan, E.V. *Roses in December: An Autobiography*. London: Galt House, 1986.

Campbell, Clarence T. "Settlement of London," *Transactions of the London and Middlesex Historical Society*, 1911.

Campbell, Clarence T. *Pioneer Days in London: Some Account of Men and Things in London before it became a city*. London: Advertiser Job Printing, 1921.

City of London Heritage Designations. London: Local Architectural Conservation Advisory Committee, 1987.

Connor, James T. H. *A Heritage of Healing: The London Health Association and Its Hospitals, 1909-1987*. London: London Health Association, 1990.

Crinklaw, Raymond K., Olga B. Bishop, and George P. Rickard. *Glanworth, Westminster Township: One hundred years of yesterday's news, today's history*. Lambeth: Crinklaw Press, 1987.

Curnoe, Greg. *Deeds/abstracts: the History of a London Lot*. Edited by Frank Davey. London: Brick Books, 1995.

Curnoe, Greg. *Deeds/Nations*. Edited by Frank Davey & Neil Ferris. London: London Chapter, Ontario Archaeological Society, 1996.

Curnoe, William Glen. *Treasured Times: A Chronology of London Public Library*. 1995.

Dictionary of Canadian Biography. (Volumes I-XIV) Toronto: University of Toronto Press, 1966-1998.

Fox, William Sherwood. *Sherwood Fox of Western: Reminiscences*. Toronto: Burns and MacEachern, 1964.

Grainger, Jennifer. *Vanished Villages of Middlesex*. Toronto: Natural Heritage, 2002.

Heard, Susan and staff at the London Public Library. *Masonville Crossroads: from Wilderness to Thriving Community*. London: London Public Library, 1996.

History of the County of Middlesex, Canada. W.A. and C.L. Goodspeed. 1889. Reprinted in 1972 by Mika Studio, Belleville, introduced and corrected by Daniel Brock.

Honey, Terrence W., ed. *London Heritage*. London: Phelps Publishing Company, 1991.

Illustrated Historical Atlas of the County of Middlesex, Ontario. Toronto: H.R. Page & Co., 1878. Reprinted in 1972 by Edward Phelps.

Kirkwood, Carrie. *A Collection from the Hamilton Road Area*. London: Carrie Kirkwood, 1997.

Kirkwood, Carrie. *The Hamilton Road Collection, Volume 2: More Memories from Old East*. London: Carrie Kirkwood, 2001.

A Lasting Treasure: London Public Library since 1895. London: London Public Library, 1994.

Lewis, Jennie Raycraft. *"Llyndinshire" — London Township*. [N.P.] 1967.

London and Its Men of Affairs, London: Advertiser Job Printing Company, Limited, n.d.

London Township: A Rich Heritage, 1796-1997. Volume I. Arva: London Township History Book Committee, 2001.

London Township: Families Past and Present. Volume II. Arva: London Township History Book Committee, 2001.

Lutman, John H. and Christopher L. Hives. *The North and the East of London: an Historical and Architectural Guide*. London: Corporation of the City of London, 1982.

Lutman, John H. *The Historic Heart of London*. London: Corporation of the City of London, 1977.

Lutman, John H. *The South and the West: an Historical and Architectural Guide*. London: Corporation of the City of London, 1979.

Middleton, Jesse Edgar and Fred Landon. *The Province of Ontario: A History, 1615-1927*. Toronto: Dominion Publishing, 1927.

Mika, Nick. *Places in Ontario: their Name Origins and History*. 3 volumes.

Belleville: Mika Publishing Company, 1977-83.

Miller, Orlo. *This was London: the First two Centuries.* Westport: Butternut Press, 1988.

Morden, Pat. *Putting Down Roots: a History of London's Parks and Rivers.* St. Catharines: Stonehouse, 1988.

Morningstar, Charles K. *From Dobbin to Diesel: The Story of Public Transportation in London, Canada.* London: London Transportation Commission, 1973.

Phillips, Glen C. *On Tap: The Odyssey of Beer and Brewing in Victorian London-Middlesex.* Sarnia: Cheshire Cat Press, 2000.

Priddis, Harriett. "The Naming of London Streets," *Transactions of the London and Middlesex Historical Society*, 1908-1909. And in its *Centennial Review, 1967.* London: London & Middlesex Historical Society, 1967.

Proudfoot, William. "The Proudfoot Papers, 1832-1848," London and Middlesex Historical Society, *Transactions*, various parts between 1915 and 1938.

Rosser, Frederick T. *London Township Pioneers: including some families from adjoining areas.* Belleville: Mika, 1975.

Seaborn, Edwin. *The March of Medicine in Western Ontario.* Toronto: Ryerson, 1944.

Shaw, Eleanor. *A History of the London Public Library.* London: London Public Library and Art Museum, 1968.

Shawyer, A.J. *Broughdale: Looking For Its Past.* London: Broughdale Community Association, 1981.

Skidmore, Patricia G. *Brescia College, 1919-1979.* London: Brescia College 1980.

St-Denis, Guy. *Byron: Pioneer Days in Westminster Township.* Lambeth: Crinklaw Press, 1985.

St-Denis, Guy, ed. *Simcoe's Choice: Celebrating London's Bicentennial.* Toronto: Dundurn Press, 1992.

Tausky, Nancy Z. *Historical Sketches of London: from Site to City.* Peterborough: Broadview Press, 1993.

Tausky, Nancy Z and Lynne D. DiStefano, *Symbols of Aspiration: Victorian Architecture in London and Southwestern Ontario.* Toronto: University of Toronto Press, 1986.

Walling, H.F., ed. *Tackabury's Atlas of the Dominion of Canada.* Montreal: G.N. Tackabury, 1876.

Women's Institute (Canada). Crumlin Branch. *Women's Institute Tweedsmuir History, Crumlin Branch, Middlesex County, Ontario, 1924-1985.* microfilm.

CONTRIBUTORS

CHRISTOPHER ANDREAE is an industrial archaeologist based in London. He is well-known as a railway historian for his book, *Lines of Country: An Atlas of Railway and Waterway History in Canada* (1997).

FREDERICK H. ARMSTRONG was educated at the University of Toronto and taught 19th century Canadian political and urban history at The University of Western Ontario. His books include *The Forest City*, a history of London.

ALEX ARTHUR was born in Scotland. He taught school and had a sixteen-year career in municipal politics in Barrie. Retired in London, he is president of the Broughdale Community Association.

MIKE BAKER is Curator of Regional History at Museum London and the editor of *Downtown London: Layers of Time* (1998).

NETTA (KINGSMILL) BRANDON, when young, listened to stories of local London families, buildings, businesses, and farms. She received the Queen's Golden Jubilee Medal for her dedication to architectural and historical conservation in 2003.

DAN BROCK, now retired from the London District Catholic School Board, has written extensively on London and area history. His works include *Best Wishes from London, Canada: Our Golden Age of Post Cards, 1903-1914.*

DR. HOWIE CAMERON is a veteran of WWII, a celebrated orthopedic surgeon, archivist of the London Hunt and Country Club, and has played with all the golfers in his story.

GLEN CURNOE recently retired as librarian of the London Room of the London Public Library after seventeen years. He continues to pursue his keen interest in local history.

GEORGE P. DEKAY, a lifelong resident of the area west of Hyde Park, is a retired London Board of Education teacher. He has published local family histories and has provided contributions for the West Williams (1999) and London (2001) township history books.

CHRISTOPHER DOTY is an award-winning documentary maker whose work includes *Lost April: The Flood of '37, The Royal Tour of 1939*, and the restoration of Canada's first feature-length colour movie, *Talbot of Canada*.

FREDERICK A. DREYER taught British history at The University of Western Ontario. He has written about Edmund Burke, the origins of Methodism, and the Moravian Missions in Canada. Fred Dreyer enjoys opera.

JIM ETHERINGTON is a London writer and communications consultant, former journalist, and co-author of *London: Claiming the Future* (2000).

DON FLECKSER is a noted London actor, director and educator. His favourite pastime is sitting on his front porch watching Franklin Ave. go by with his son Martin and labs Ben and Fred.

ALICE GIBB has edited township histories of Huron, Lambton, and Middlesex Counties. Her interest in history was derived from her mother, who wrote the Tweedsmuir History for the Froomfield Women's Institute.

JENNIFER GRAINGER was trained in archaeology at the University of Toronto and the University of London, England. She is the author of *Vanished Villages of Middlesex*, and has contributed several chapters for Middlesex township histories.

DENIS HAMMOND immigrated to Canada in 1948. For twenty-five years (1962-87), he was Senior Subdivision Planner for the City of London, and was responsible for the name of every street in that period.

A. M. J. HYATT studied at the Royal Military College, and at the University of Toronto, Carleton, and Duke Universities. He taught military history at The University of Western Ontario, and is the biographer of Sir Arthur Currie.

MAUREEN ZUNTI JONES graduated from the University of Calgary with a Masters in Environmental Design. She is a planner with Stantec Consulting in London.

DOUGLAS LEIGHTON was educated at McMaster University, The University of Western Ontario, and Huron University College, and has been a member of the History Department at Huron since 1973.

ANN MCCOLL LINDSAY is a graduate in Honours English from the University of Windsor. Her articles on urban issues have appeared in newspapers, magazines and books. Market districts are her primary interest.

ARTHUR MCCLELLAND is Librarian of the London Room and secretary of the Historic Sites Committee of the London Public Library Board. He has written on collecting local and genealogical materials.

G. CAMPBELL MCDONALD is a 1949 journalism graduate from The University of Western Ontario, whose career embraced newspapers, radio, TV, university and government communications and teaching. Now retired in Toronto, he was a Londoner for twenty-five years.

ALAN MACEACHERN directs the Public History program at The University of Western Ontario, and has published *Natural Selections: National Parks in Atlantic Canada 1935-1970* (2001), and *The Institute of Man & Resources: An Environmental Fable* (2003).

CATHERINE (MAINE) MCEWEN was born and educated in London. After graduating from The University of Western Ontario, she married and raised a family. An abiding interest in history has culminated in a book, *No Smiling Path.*

ANNE MCKILLOP taught history, and was a founder of the Heritage London Foundation and the local chapter of the Architectural Conservancy of Ontario. She helped prepare London's *Inventory of Heritage Buildings* (2001).

GRANT MALTMAN is a London resident who remembers when Banting Crescent was a field. As curator of Banting House National Historic Site, he has published a number of articles on Sir Frederick Banting.

JOHN MOMBOURQUETTE is principal of John Paul II Catholic Secondary School and has an avid interest in local history. He has served on the boards of several community organizations, including two terms as president of the London and Middlesex Historical Society.

HILARY BATES NEARY is a volunteer with written, spoken, and sung words. She researches pioneer mills on the Thames, and lives at the corner of Regent Street and Lombardo Avenue.

PETER NEARY is Professor of History and former Dean of Social Science at The University of Western Ontario. Both a Newfoundlander and Ontarian, he has written on the history of his two provinces.

ALASTAIR NEELY is Librarian at the Westmount branch of the London Public Library. He is curator of London's First Hussars Museum and is skilled in genealogical research.

NANCY GEDDES POOLE, former Executive Director of the London Regional Art and Historical Museums, is a graduate of The University of Western Ontario, from which she also received an LL D in 1990. She is the author of *The Art of London 1830-1980* (1984).

THERESA REGNIER assists researchers at the J.J. Talman Regional Collection, The University of Western Ontario. She is a member of Landmarks London, the London Advisory Committee on Heritage, and the Archives Association of Ontario.

A.J. SHAWYER, PhD, is currently an Associate Professor of Geography at the Memorial University of Newfoundland. Jo grew up in London, Ontario. Her research into cultural landscapes includes *Broughdale: Looking for Its Past* (1981, 2nd ed. 1994), the history of a London neighbourhood.

DAVID R. SPENCER is a Professor in the Faculty of Information and Media Studies at The University of Western Ontario. He currently (2003-04) holds the Rogers Chair for Studies in Journalism and New Media.

NANCY TAUSKY is a Professor of English at The University of Western Ontario and the author of *Historical Sketches of London: from Site to City* (1993) and *Symbols of Aspiration: Victorian Architecture in London and Southwestern Ontario* (1986).

NEVILLE THOMPSON teaches at The University of Western Ontario, and has published *The Anti-Appeasers: Conservative Opposition to Appeasement in the 1930s* (1971), *Wellington After Waterloo* (1986), and *Earl Bathurst and the British Empire 1762-1834* (1999).

JONATHAN VANCE holds a Canada Research Chair at The University of Western Ontario, and has published *Death So Noble: Memory, Meaning, and the First World War* (1997) and *High Flight: Aviation and the Canadian Imagination* (2002).

P.B. WAITE is Professor Emeritus of History at Dalhousie University, and is an Officer of the Order of Canada.

INDEX